CW00336443

Praise for *Valued at Work*

As we aim to get more women into careers in STEM industries, we can't let them down by then allowing them to face toxic working cultures. As a woman reading this book, I recognise so many of the behaviours called out, and know many other women who would, too. There are some great tips in here to help you push back when faced with things a man simply wouldn't be asked to do, let alone tolerate, most probably. But ultimately this is a book that men need to read. You may recognise some of the poor behaviours called out in yourself and others, and I applaud and thank any man that picks up this book to educate themselves. I ask you then to get a copy for a friend and be more 'Markus' and hold more 'Steves' to account to help shape a workplace that enables more women to flourish.

Samantha Niblett, Founder of Labour: Women in Tech

This is a great read; the scenarios Lauren highlights are very powerful (and sometimes cringeworthy) examples of what really happens in organisations and which must continue to be addressed. I absolutely love the 'top tips' sections and will be revisiting these!

Lisa Waterhouse, Head of UK Diversity, Equity, and Inclusion, National Grid

A very interesting format for male allies to learn how they can support women in the workplace! A great and easy read addressing much-needed conversations around inclusion – five stars!

Vanessa Vallely OBE, Founder and CEO, WeAreTheCity and WeAreTechWomen

A fantastic read, where Lauren Neal expertly dissects a topic which is fundamental to our time, providing a road map for how we can create meaningful change. By using a really interesting approach of case studying two approaches (no doubt being played out for real every single day in workplaces around the world), Lauren shines a light on the nuances that exist within these issues that can become such obstacles to progress, and so provides a really useful resource for those seeking education in this area. Without question, essential reading for every male leader who aspires to ethical inclusive leadership.

Richard Pickard, CEO, Inclusive Search Ltd

Lauren Neal is a true champion for women working in the challenging field of STEM. Her book gives incredible insights into gender equity and career progression for women in this field through her engaging with the dialogue of men in this male-dominated arena and their views and behaviour. One realises from the book that the motivation for making changes is critical to sustaining action and planning outcomes – it definitely leaves us with hope for the future.

Pinky Lilani CBE DL, Founder and Chairperson of Women of the Future Programme

This is a powerful book that everyone involved in hiring, developing, and managing people should read. Brought to life by real experiences of behaviours happening now, affecting the attraction, retention, and development of female engineers. Until these experiences are addressed and transformed we will never be able to create the equitable engineering sector that we will all thrive in. This book will enable change by addressing unconscious bias and demonstrating the reality of being a female engineer today. Thank you for writing it!

Natalie Desty, Founder of STEM Returners

Outstanding! This is the book that I wish I had at the start of my allyship journey. A refreshingly practical and non-judgemental guide for anyone looking to become an active ally.

Lee Chambers, Psychologist and Founder of Essentialise Workplace Wellbeing

A powerful blend of story, insight, and advice. This is an unusual book about an important topic: woven through the story of two fictional male leaders trying to address bias at work are stories which will resonate with women in STEM, along with advice for organisations. Easy to read – and well worth reading!

Kathryn Bishop CBE, Associate Fellow at the Saïd Business School, University of Oxford

Lauren Neal has written a must-read provocative, pragmatic, and realistic account for anyone curious about addressing biases in today's workforce, where far too many women are still struggling to find their 'space'. These conversations between Steve and Markus, two managers working in a male-dominated environment, trigger (or create) a strong feeling of déjà vu, a sense of urgency, and a powerful call to action. A journey into the 'rock 'n' roll' world of women in the energy and other male-dominated sectors!

Nadia Lalout-Landemaine, Deputy Co-chair of LEAN IN Equity & Sustainability

Lauren Neal's book is a highly refreshing take on finding solutions to the real issues many STEM-driven businesses face from a lack of women entering and staying in their sector and in their organisations. She explores what can be done to address the issues through the eyes of Steve and Markus, two fictional middle-ranking male managers who want to see change. They are both struggling with the day-to-day challenges of advancing women in STEM, assessing what they can do and actually trying some things to make a difference. The combination of their dialogue as they share their experiences, Lauren's narrative, and her top tips for organisations and STEM women are really insightful, and will inspire new thinking and action to address this seemingly intractable problem.

Robert Baker, CEO, Potentia Talent Consulting Ltd

What caught my attention in Lauren's book is the presentation of the topic of gender equity in STEM. It is really original how, using reciprocal mentoring meetings of two executives, she conveys key obstacles faced by STEM women. Markus and Steve spend a year sharing experiences and advice on gender equity for women in STEM, but it is the author who is sharing her own thoughts: clever, very clever. There is a huge amount of experience and research shared on obstacles facing gender equity for women in STEM, from recruitment to development, and promotion.

Joana Visa, PCC, PhD, Founder of VISA Coaching Institute

Valued at Work is required reading for every professional, especially those in global leadership roles. Data continues to prove that qualified and talented women continue to leave STEM roles at record levels throughout the globe. Neal takes the reader through an inspiring and sometimes frustrating journey on recognising, understanding, and taking corrective action surrounding biases (known and unknown), the value and importance of diversity and inclusion, and ultimately the responsibility we each have in ensuring equality for all. Her real-life examples take a 360-degree approach to identifying misconceptions, finding advocates, creating support and community understanding, and suggestions for company and leadership change management. Neal also offers women in STEM steps to take in order to further their careers, avoid burnout, and ultimately feel valued at work. Women in STEM are lucky to have Neal as an advocate, and I can't wait to share this book with my leadership team!

Alexian Wines, Chief Operating Officer, BowerGroupAsia, and international motivational speaker

Valued at Work is a must-read book for anyone who believes in gender equality and wants to see more women succeed in their careers. This inspiring and thought-provoking book sheds light on the numerous challenges that women face in the workplace and offers practical solutions for overcoming them. Through insightful anecdotes, compelling research, and real-world examples, author Lauren Neal makes a compelling case for why valuing women is not only the right thing to do but also makes good business sense. Overall, *Valued at Work* is a powerful call to action for organisations and individuals. It challenges us to recognise the value of women's contributions and to take concrete steps to create a more inclusive and equitable workplace for all. I highly recommend this book to all those in leadership roles.

Jim Carbaugh, MEd, educational leader, TEDx speaker, and coach

This book enthrals readers through a compelling dialogue and transformative mentorship journey between two men, allowing us to discern their contrasting approaches and draw our own conclusions. As a woman who has experienced the challenges of working in male-dominated environments, I found great resonance in the stories shared, and the clarity of the tips offered proved immensely valuable. What sets this book apart is its emphasis on constructive advice rather than dwelling on gender equality complaints, offering valuable guidance for women to proactively carve out successful careers and gain a strong foothold in their professional journey.

Adeline Lim, SVP and Deputy Head of Risk Management, BOC Aviation

Prepare to be inspired by this thought-provoking book on inclusion of women at work. Through the engaging narrative of two men, it explores the intersection of personal motivation and business outcomes in fostering inclusivity. Their real-life stories paint a vivid picture of the challenges faced by women in the workplace. With examples and actionable strategies, Lauren brilliantly sparks reflection and equips readers with practical insights towards a more inclusive culture. A captivating read that will be a catalyst for change for individuals and organisations to champion gender equality and create workplaces where everyone can thrive.

Berrak Banu Kurt, SVP and Head of People and Culture, Volvo Group

Valued at Work is a must-read for those wanting to bridge the gender gap at work. Lauren has first-hand experience of navigating a successful career in a male-dominated work environment. This book shines a light on the challenges many women still face in not just the energy and tech industries but across many industries globally. The real-world examples and actionable advice packed throughout the chapters are a particular highlight. *Valued at Work* will not only educate you on the imbalance of inclusion in the workplace but equip you with strategies to create real change.

Marielle Legair, speaker, LinkedIn Top Voice and LinkedIn Learning Instructor

Improving gender balance in STEM is an aspiration in many corporate strategies. Leaders are encouraged to build inclusive cultures in their teams by showcasing the benefits on offer. The negatives of a noninclusive culture don't get as much airtime. *Valued at Work* explores why learning through empathy might be the best way to change a culture and why what a leader 'hears' really matters. Lauren outlines experiences that women in STEM may face as they progress in their careers. Her story shows the good and bad in a captivating account of how two leaders 'lean in' to their corporate strategies.

Mike Smith, Wells Superintendent, and winner of WeAreTheCity Rising Stars 2023: Men for Gender Balance

Lauren has expertly crafted a compelling narrative that sheds light on the challenges that women face in STEM careers and offers practical strategies to overcome biases and create a more equitable workplace. One of *Valued at Work*'s greatest strengths is its emphasis on tangible solutions as Lauren not only highlights the various forms of bias that women encounter, but also provides readers with a toolkit of strategies and best practices to address and mitigate these biases to foster inclusivity and create environments where women can thrive. What sets this book apart, however, is its intersectional lens: Lauren recognises that women's experiences in STEM are shaped by multiple dimensions of identity, including race, ethnicity, and socio-economic background, and offers a nuanced and comprehensive perspective that recognises the unique challenges faced by women from diverse backgrounds. Furthermore, it presents a compelling case for the business imperative of gender diversity in STEM as Lauren highlights the research and evidence that demonstrate the numerous benefits of diverse teams, including increased innovation, improved problem-solving, and enhanced organisational performance. *Valued at Work* is a vital resource for individuals, organisations, and leaders committed to creating inclusive and equitable environments by dismantling bias, championing diversity, and empowering women in STEM.

Prachi Garg, Author of *Superwomen*

As a woman working in a male-dominated industry myself, I am thrilled to endorse *Valued at Work* because as someone who has navigated these hurdles myself, I found her insights to be incredibly empowering. This groundbreaking book tackles the all too familiar challenges of feeling invisible, frustrated, and undervalued in traditionally male-dominated workplaces. *Valued at Work* is a game changer, offering approaches based on real life experiences that enable organisations to foster gender equity without alienating any segment of their workforce. Neal's expertise as an award-winning professional in her industry shines through as she shares tangible solutions to drive real change and make her an exceptional guide for women in any male-dominated industry. Her emphasis on inclusivity, diversity, and the value of every individual's contributions is both refreshing and essential for transforming workplace culture. I wholeheartedly recommend *Valued at Work* to all women working in male-dominated fields, as well as to leaders, managers, and organisations committed to fostering inclusivity and diversity. This book will inspire you, equip you with practical tools, and empower you to create lasting change.

Zinet Kemal, Award-winning Cybersecurity Practitioner and Author of *See Yourself in Cybersecurity*

A must-read for every male leader who works in STEM and wants to be a truly inclusive leader. I love the way the book follows two very different journeys, clearly highlighting the benefits of leaning into inclusion and diversity and becoming a better ally and agent of change. The book contains really practical actions which should benefit every leader.

Daniele Fiandaca, Founder, Token Man Consulting

Valued at Work is an incredibly powerful read, especially if you think you are well versed in the unconscious and conscious bias that continues to infiltrate our workplaces. It serves as a reminder that we are still very much in the middle of this journey to acknowledge and really see STEM women and the power and value they bring to any organisation. It is written with authenticity, and the experiences are not only relatable, they repeat themselves time and again, even in 2023. It's not just what's said, it's what's not said and how women feel on a nearly daily basis. From 'admin girls' to 'office housework' to leaders truly needing to become 'people people', Lauren does a fantastic job of coaching both organisations and individuals into stepping into the uncomfortable space of taking accountability for what happens today and the improvements we need to make together.

Stacy Ross, VP Operations, Former USAF Pilot, Engineer

As I read *Valued at Work* I felt so many emotions – namely, frustration but also hope. Frustration because so many women experience the feeling of not being seen or heard, valued, or visible. Hope because this book highlights the conversations that need to be happening and need to be happening right NOW! Lauren Neal has given us an insight into how STEM women are treated in their workplace. Her expert tips and strategies educate both women and organisations on how to overcome the deeply and downright soul-destroying experiences for STEM women. Being seen and heard runs through me, it's in my blood to fight for women who are quietened and whose lights are dimmed by others around them; this is a perfect example of how we can start bringing around the changes in sexist, discriminatory behaviours that need to happen for every single woman today.

Nicki James, CEO, Personal Brand Strategist and Bestselling Author

Valued at Work shines a much-needed light on gender bias and equity. Through the enlightening dialogue of two men, Lauren opens a powerful window into the intricate dynamics of gender bias. The book offers invaluable insights for reflection and practical tools to challenge the status quo, foster change, and champion more equitable and inclusive organisations. Prepare to be informed, inspired, and empowered!

Martin Solway and Fidel Torreiro, Co-founders of The Audax Generation

VALUED
AT
WORK

SHINING A LIGHT ON BIAS TO ENGAGE,
ENABLE, AND RETAIN WOMEN IN STEM

LAUREN NEAL

First published in Great Britain by Practical Inspiration Publishing, 2023

© Lauren Neal, 2023

The moral rights of the author have been asserted

ISBN   9781788604680   (print)
      9781788604703   (epub)
      9781788604697   (mobi)

Every effort has been made to trace copyright holders and to obtain their permission for the use of copyright material. The publisher apologises for any errors or omissions and would be grateful if notified of any corrections that should be incorporated in future reprints or editions of this book.

Want to bulk-buy copies of this book for your team and colleagues? We can customise the content and co-brand *Valued at Work* to suit your business's needs.

Please email info@practicalinspiration.com for details.

To Mum and Dad – thank you for always supporting me to
be whatever I choose in life;
Gemma and Kristian – our bond will never break;
Isabella and Gabriella – keep bringing the
wagging-tail joy every day;
and Umber – thank you for being by my side through the
good and bad, and never giving up.

To all the women who feel invisible, overlooked, and
frustrated at work – you are not alone.
And to all their employing organisations…
start seeing them.

Table of contents

Foreword

When Lauren asked me to write the foreword for her book, I was excited to do it. I witnessed the birth of her thoughts around the topics of diversity and inclusion when she was young and observed them through to today – I would often call her a 'collector of waifs and strays', as Lauren never liked to see anyone excluded.

I am a woman of pensionable age and I am extremely proud of my three adult children. I have two daughters who strive daily to promote others and a son who tutors students from all walks of life through their competencies to earn their charterships. My husband is English – he could be seen as a straight white alpha male with the privilege that goes with it; however, he was born into a southeast London home, sharing a community with various cultures. I was born in Trinidad and Tobago, and arrived in Southampton, England, in 1960, as did many of the Windrush generation who had been encouraged to come to England for work. My brother, sister, and I were sent here by my grandparents to be reunited with my parents who had arrived a few years before us, as my father was at university. I clearly remember shivering with cold and thinking how different this was to my sunny, warm Caribbean home. I was four years old.

Looking back now, I can see how recognition of diversity and the benefits that it gives us was so needed. While London was swinging and adjusting to the influences of different cultures, there were glaring discrepancies in how ordinary people were treated: Black people were often referred to in derogatory terms, Indian people would change or shorten their name to make it easier and less demeaning when some people could not pronounce it – there were lots of Bobs and Daves. Employment opportunities were limited, and many application forms were binned with the excuse being one of 'nobody could say that', and very few people of colour made it into offices. With the establishment of the Commission for Racial Equality (1970s), we have seen small improvements.

Like many others, I had various name-calling incidents, mindless individuals who copied the behaviours of the bullies of society. I qualified with two degrees, social sciences and social work, and I have worked with various councils assisting children of all ages, including adolescents, and latterly supporting the fostering community by providing training, recruitment, and supervision of foster carers.

Lauren's father, who works in the energy industry, provided her with invaluable insights from his diverse career, ranging from commercial diving to delivering an extensive range of projects as director. The recognition of the generational shift enabled them to see the workplace through each other's eyes, and highlighted the limitations of the strategies that had worked for her father but were inadequate for Lauren's reality.

To gather her material, Lauren spoke with many people inside and outside her industry. Often, we would have discussions over the dinner table and FaceTime, debating what would be included, as the subject matter is unfortunately vast. Key aspects of bias in *Valued at Work*, such as race, age, religion, sexual orientation, class, and disability, have deliberately been left ambiguous and open to interpretation. Today, these biases are indirect and direct microaggressions that can leave women reflecting if it is really happening.

As a woman of mixed race, throughout her career Lauren has experienced various incidents professionally, giving her a unique perspective that she shares within the pages of this book and through Steve and Markus. Lauren uses dialogue to show it is possible to open your mind to looking at other possible ways of expressing and implementing equity in the workplaces of competent women. Steve and Markus contrast each other, each harbouring a different train of thought when it comes to the subject matter. Markus looks at it for the long term, foreseeing what he sees happening now projecting into the future that his daughter will face as she enters the workplace. This is his impetus for change. Steve's thought processes evolve around the situation as it stands. He is competent at being able to communicate that change is imminent while maintaining the status quo.

Cultural diversity, inclusion, addressing bias and unconscious bias, and valuing people for their skills and experience is an ongoing battle, both for the employer and the employee. Women's roles in the workplace have for generations been unseen and undervalued. It has taken years and immeasurable courage from women all over the world, using whatever medium was available to them, to raise the possibility of equality. Looking at history, Emmeline Pankhurst's achievements enabled women to take up the baton in the quest for living in a just and enabling society that you would want your daughters to thrive in. In today's world, women are still fighting systems that restrict their choices – for example, health choices and workplace politics that favour a patriarchal system that casts women primarily in a support role.

We must acknowledge the inspiring, brave, and forward-thinking women who have made their mark in history by pushing the envelope. My personal heroes come from all walks of life: Rosa Parks, Michelle Obama, Malala Yousafzai, Greta Thunberg, and Ruth Bader Ginsburg, to name a few. There are so many more women making a real difference to the lives of women in this society that go unnoticed.

Through her book, Lauren encourages both the employee and employer to take an honest look at practices in the work-place, encouraging discussion on the practicality of cultural change, societal change, and the evolution in thinking about the value of people. Lauren clearly identifies the importance of this staying on everyone's mind – how we treat each other has to be open to change or we are destined to repeat it.

It has been over 80 years since the end of World War II. Many of our societal norms were implemented favouring the patriarchal structures that were identified as the way our society should develop. Women were not seen as equal to men and their roles were limited to the home and vocational employment. How a woman conducted herself, what she wore, and who she socialised with was open to scrutiny by her family and community. Women were assigned a role and were expected to keep to it. Women have struggled in many arenas over many years to claim equity, and unfortunately, as Lauren has identified, the fight will go on. The hope is that changes will come and women will claim their rightful place as equals with abilities and dreams that can match any man's.

Seeta Neal
Lauren's mother

Preface

Imagine you are the only person who is different in the room. When you finally get your voice heard, you're met with silence.

The discussion then moves on as though you had said nothing. You are only called on to share slides or to take notes, even though you have skills and experience that no one else in the room has.

You feel invisible, undervalued, and frustrated, and think regularly about resigning.

And when organisational leaders speak about diversity, equity, and inclusion, they talk about recruitment of new employees – not retaining or valuing existing ones.

Women in STEM experience this. Every. Single. Day.

A lot of people assume women leave the workplace due to child or family caring responsibilities. But a lot of women are leaving not because of that. They are leaving due to toxic workplace cultures.

How do I know that? I have experienced it myself – multiple times.

I was regularly questioning my skills and abilities, and what I needed to do to 'fit in'.

This is happening right now, not 20 years ago.

It can be more difficult than you may think to find someone who understands the challenges. But it doesn't need to stay this way.

Valued at Work explores these topics in a very human way – overhearing the conversations between two business leaders through a 'fly-on-the-wall' perspective. Steve and Markus are trying genuinely to improve retention of women in their respective organisations. While they discuss the problems that women face within the patriarchal system, with concrete examples, they are actively trying to understand and change it.

They get it right, and they get it wrong.

This fictional approach to a real business problem allows you, the reader, to empathise with these male organisational leaders in their own struggles, as well as with the women in theirs, with less judgement than is typical when discussing this topic.

It is time to re-evaluate how we value women in STEM and their contributions, particularly in male-dominated sectors like energy and technology. This needs to change now while we have very real challenges whereby diversity of thought would unlock new solutions – for example, solving the trilemma of clean, affordable, and secure energy, or balancing cybersecurity with privacy.

Businesses need to refocus on engaging, enabling, and retaining women in STEM through a culture whereby authentic humility is promoted and valued to create truly diverse teams. Diverse teams drive the much greater innovation that is needed for the world today, reach better business outcomes for their organisations, and reduce attrition.

This can be achieved in three steps by:

1. Acknowledging your organisation's behaviours.
2. Including the right technical skills and recognising performance – particularly for women in STEM.
3. Empowering your future leaders.

And the best part? All this is possible without alienating any of the workforce.

While the lessons in this book are based on many real-world experiences, my own and others', the names, characters, businesses, places, events, and incidents presented in the coming pages are fictitious, and should not be interpreted as corresponding to any specific situation or individual persons.

Acknowledgements

There are many people who have inspired and supported the process of creating *Valued at Work*. While there are too many to name, some shining lights include:

- My mum for sharing her experiences in the foreword and drawing parallels to today's continued challenges in DEI. And of course all the late night chapter reviews and deep, thought-provoking discussions on workplace culture and society - they made a lasting impact.
- Umber – who encouraged me to reframe my experiences into something positive and without whom *Valued at Work* wouldn't have been written.
- The courageous women in STEM who shared their stories with me.
- My fantastic beta readers whose feedback was invaluable: Kathryn Bishop CBE; Jim Carbaugh; Paul Hollis; Catherine Podesta; Robert Baker; Narmin Zulfugarova; and Mike Smith.
- Alison Jones and her fabulous team at Practical Inspiration Publishing, and Newgen Publishing UK, for all their support and guidance as I navigated this process from the Business Book Proposal Challenge through to release.

- The following trailblazers who fearlessly stand up for the change we want to see in the world: Helen Murray, Caitlin McCall, Ada Elliott, Christina Tueje, Lily Keisler, Tracy Sharp, Sara Passone, Hui See Yap, Stacy Ross, Angeni Jayawickramarajah, Nicki James, Lamé Verre, Nadia Lalout-Landemaine, every single person on the 2022 Oxford Women Transforming Leadership Programmes, and the Evolution Mastermind.
- And those with whom I've found my people including: Claire Gray, Sarah McColl, Trung Le, Hazem Fayad, Esmira Qudratova, Nigar Salmanova, Kiana Sinclair, Zinet Kemal, Akua Opong, Karl Lowe, Daniel Eggert, Shandelle Hosein, Fatema Kassam, Zeena Adnan, and Portia Waddell.

Thank you.

Introduction

At an awards ceremony in December for women in STEM (Science, Technology, Engineering, Mathematics), two men from different companies meet and start a conversation. Steve and Markus work for organisations in the energy and tech sectors, and were invited to attend the ceremony as guests of sponsors.

Steve works in the tech sector and has been very successful in his career, reaching his current position reporting directly to the CEO. Steve's organisation has worked hard to attract women in STEM and is proud to now have on average a 1:1 ratio of male to female employees at junior levels. This ratio reduces to 30:1 at senior levels – addressing this is on their improvement plan. Lately, Steve has noticed a high turnover of female staff – particularly in STEM roles. There is an ongoing recruitment drive to replace those who have left which is becoming costly. Recently some high-potential women have left the company and while Steve is worried that there is an underlying reason for their exits, his primary concern is the continued reduction in profits. Last quarter, his organisation lost two high-profile customers who stated it was due to lack of innovative solutions, and one unofficially advised they were reshaping their portfolio to include a more diverse supply chain to unlock new ways of thinking. Steve thinks of himself as a reasonable and professional man, and has worked with teams of men in his organisation throughout his career, but it is clear to him that the organisation needs to modernise or it will be left behind.

Markus works in the energy sector. He started his career working on offshore platforms around the world and now is a senior leader in his organisation. Markus's organisation has also achieved a 1:1 average male to female ratio of employees at junior levels and at the most senior level. However, at middle management level, the ratio sits around 40:1 male to female for STEM roles. Markus is an executive sponsor for his organisation's gender-focused employee resource group (ERG). He meets with the team once per quarter (his calendar permitting) and hears a lot about initiatives to build networks and keynote speaking sessions from leaders in other parts of the business. Markus is unsure how these initiatives meet the needs of the business, but wants to enable the group to define their own mission and objectives. While Markus is very focused on work, he is also a father to six-year-old Isabella and beams whenever he speaks about her. Isabella's favourite subject at school is mathematics, and she loves playing with Lego®. She said that when she grows up she wants to be an engineer, and Markus wants Isabella to have every opportunity for this to happen. He would be so proud for her to have a career in STEM.

The evening at the ceremony consisted of several presentations and speeches from industry experts and leaders. One quote stood out from an anonymous woman in STEM that was shown on screen:

'I feel invisible. Like everyone is turning their back on me and forgetting I exist. It's this feeling in the pit of my stomach that makes my throat feel more hollow. I close my eyes, take a deep breath, and just get on with it, knowing this is only Tuesday.'

It was clear to both Steve and Markus that to be a woman in a traditionally male-dominated industry is to be a trail-blazer, but they always thought women felt positively challenged and thrilled to be making a difference. Both of them wondered if women within their respective organisations felt like that.

Many of the presenters called out current statistics in STEM:

- Less than 27% of the STEM workforce are female in the UK (WISE, 2022) and the US (US Census Bureau, 2021).
- Energy employs 65 million people globally (IEA, 2022). Women account for 22% of employees in the oil and gas industry in 2020 (Von Lonski, et al., 2021).
- The decline in representation as women progress from mid-career positions to more senior roles exceeds 50% (Von Lonski, et al., 2021).
- Women in technical and operational roles in energy represent 12% at mid-career and 9% at senior level (Von Lonski, et al., 2021).

- Over 50% of women in oil and gas feel that sponsorship is an important pathway to promotion and senior-level advancement (Von Lonski, et al., 2021).
- 58% of women in energy said their company has formal sponsorship but only 12% were benefiting from it (Cairnie and Muscat, 2022).
- For women in energy, regular coaching from supervisors and having a senior sponsor to help find opportunities were the most powerful factors in boosting their perception of the likelihood of their advancement (Cairnie and Muscat, 2022).
- Women are leaving the workforce at record levels (LeanIn.Org and McKinsey, 2022).

Steve and Markus meet each other in the foyer halfway through the ceremony. They discuss and reflect on the statistics and stories they heard that evening and are concerned at how frequently women in STEM feel undervalued at work.

Steve thought about the high-potential women leaving his organisation – Why did they really leave? What could've made them stay? What could he do to prevent more leaving?

Markus thought about Isabella and about what needs to happen today to ensure that she will have an equitable experience when she enters the workforce. He also considered his ERG and why he hadn't heard these stories through that initiative.

Both men want to take action. They commit to 'leaning in' and to making changes in their respective organisations.

At the end of the ceremony, they meet again and agree on three key topics to address: organisational behaviours, inclusion of hidden skills, and empowerment of future leaders. They agree to meet quarterly by means of reciprocal mentoring sessions to support each other and share ideas.

After the awards ceremony, Steve met with his line manager to discuss what he had heard and his concerns about what he is seeing in the business. He proposed an initiative that he would chair to dig into how women in STEM feel and how they are treated within the organisation.

Steve included this as part of his annual performance plan for the upcoming year:

Objective:

Increase the number of customers through the creation of diverse teams delivering innovative solutions.

Measures:

Reduce recruitment and training spending through improvement in motivation and reduced attrition of women in STEM.

Increase the number of contracted customers compared with the previous year.

Hold quarterly reciprocal mentorship meetings to share best practices to drive further improvements in motivating and retaining women in STEM.

Steve leaves for his year-end holidays committed to improving business the following year.

At his next meeting with his leadership team, Markus shared his reflections from the awards ceremony. Of his team of two women and nine men, only two (one woman and one man) spoke up and confirmed Markus's suspicion that women in STEM in their organisation may not all feel valued at work. The remainder of his team did not contribute to the discussion – Markus noticed.

Markus then met with the leads of his ERG and had a very constructive discussion listening to their initiative plans for the following year. Markus shared his reflections from the awards ceremony and committed to prioritising meetings with the group and requested a change of meeting frequency to monthly. The leads were pleasantly surprised and felt a new sense of energy from their sponsor.

During his holidays, Markus helps Isabella with her Lego® and talks with her about what she wants to be when she grows up. She says she wants to be a scientist, but children at school told her that was a man's job. Markus tells her she can be anything she wants to be, and he will do all he can to help her. When he puts her to bed that night, he promises himself to start driving change within his own organisation and go from there.

***

Reciprocal mentoring is when both parties support each other equally and draw on their own skills and experiences to support the other. It can be very beneficial for both parties as both sides can be vulnerable – showing where they need help as well as when they are able to offer support to their co-mentor.

In this case, we have Steve and Markus. Both are professionals working in corporate organisations that are male-dominated. They have experienced an event that has driven them to take action to improve gender equity in their organisation. However, their drivers are clearly different. Markus is motivated by his emotional connection to his daughter to make a change to support her choice for her future career, whereas Steve's drivers are much more business-orientated to improve performance as well as to meet his objectives as agreed with his manager.

Over time, the impact from both Steve and Markus will be observed. Motivations for making changes are critical in order sustain action plans and achieve outcomes. With a clear driver that can be communicated to others, that they can empathise with and get behind, change is more likely to succeed. The questions for now are, can Markus's and Steve's organisations empathise with the need for change? Do they recognise the talent that already exists in their organisations that is not being developed? And do they know how leaders can make a difference in this space?

PART 1

ACKNOWLEDGE YOUR ORGANISATION'S BEHAVIOURS

Once back to work in the new year, Markus spent some time identifying women in STEM within his organisation that he either knew already or knew were active in promoting diversity, equity, and inclusion (DEI). He identified 10 women to speak with including three who are external to his organisation, and once a week he set aside time to have a conversation about their experiences.

When Steve went back to work, he continued business as usual. He held his monthly leadership team meetings, monthly meetings about personnel, and signed off any requests for recruitment. Steve met with his HR manager who raised to him that more women in STEM were leaving the organisation than joining the organisation. Steve then suggested they employ a specialist recruitment company to help improve their statistics.

Three months later in March, Steve and Markus meet in person at Markus's offices for their first session.

***

'Steve! Great to see you! How are you doing?'

'I'm very well, Markus. Now, last December we agreed to try out this reciprocal mentoring. I have some material to share, but would you like to go first?'

'That sounds great, Steve. I've learned a lot in the past few months about my organisation in general, the culture we have today compared with where we want to be, and that's as well as what I've discovered about the women in STEM within my organisation. It was quite surprising what I learned – the women are saying men like us just don't "get it".'

'We don't get what?'

'Well, everyone wants to be accepted for who they are – at work and at home. I've done some reading on this and it seems that workplace culture is the most frequent reason given by employees, and in particular women, for leaving a company. It could be management, their colleagues, their environment, and lack of flexible working.'

Steve rolled his eyes. He didn't hear men complaining about those things – why would women need to be treated any differently? He waited for Markus to finish.

'They say those aspects are often overlooked in favour of a culture driven to "win" regardless of the likely significant impacts to a worker's mental health.'

'Businesses need to make money,' Steve replied. 'Without the business being successful, there are no employees to make these comments.'

'But there have been reports about good cultures within businesses that have led to improved profits,' Markus added.

'Well, that's something worth looking into. My organisation makes sure we've got the right people at the top to make sure they're focusing on the right things. We all know behaviours are driven from the top and junior employees follow. Leaders set the tone.'

'Yes, exactly. Junior employees look to their leaders to see what is accepted, tolerated, promoted, and encouraged. And those behaviours have a ripple effect throughout an organisation, whether intentional or not. What I found very interesting is that a man and a woman behaving in similar ways can be perceived very differently.'

'How so?' Steve asked. 'Why does it matter who says it if it's the right thing to say?'

'I spoke with a few women in my organisation and they spoke about alpha males and how that is the traditional view of leadership. You know: self-confident and opinionated, high performance expectations for himself and others, highly disciplined, and unemotional.'

'That sounds about right, but I know some women like that, too, although usually women are more into the touchy-feely stuff.'

'Have you heard the term "alpha females"? It's like alpha males, except women, of course. Well, what makes them different based on what I've heard is that alpha females often value interpersonal relationships and the feelings of their colleagues higher than those other traits,' Markus replied.

'I'm not sure that's a good thing.'

This time it was Markus who sighed. He could tell Steve was unaware of his biases based on some of his comments. He didn't want to criticise him just as their relationship was building, but made a mental note to call him out on this in future meetings.

'I think there can be a middle ground. But what I found fascinating was how people speak about alpha males compared with alpha females. In companies like mine and I suppose yours, they say men can get away with being aggressive and bullying, whereas when a woman does the same, they are heavily criticised for it.'

'But surely you're not suggesting we condone bullying?'

'Oh, not at all,' Markus replied, 'but it doesn't mean it doesn't happen.'

'Well, not in my company.'

Markus remembered reading an article about how senior management and junior employees often have very different experiences within the same organisation. He could tell that Steve has strong views about the culture of his company, but wondered if he has ever talked about it with those in much lower positions than his own. He is quite sure Steve has blind spots.

'Anyway, the studies say men who lead thrive on conflict, but women are less comfortable with conflict and therefore take a more indirect approach for finding solutions. Unfortunately, this is where the contrast comes in again. She thinks she's being diplomatic, but men think she's playing politics.'

'Yes, I know a few of those politician types. You never know what they're really up to.'

'And that's one of the issues shown in the studies. Because men don't understand where they're coming from, women then start to question themselves and their abilities – this happens a lot with women.'

'Really? Don't they have confidence in themselves?' Steve couldn't understand why women wouldn't feel confident in their abilities. He has never experienced that, and couldn't think of any men he's worked with ever mentioning feeling like that.

'I think it's more than just self-confidence, Steve.' Markus remembered several conversations where women told him they had felt excluded, sometimes subtly and sometimes very obviously. 'Apparently this happens a lot to women with diverse perspectives. They come up with innovative solutions, but are not often in a position where people value their perspectives and they get left out.'

Steve thought about diverse perspectives and the feedback from his recent supply chain discussions. 'Diversity is something we need to promote more – particularly in the current climate. Customers are looking to diversify their supply chain, so it looks like another box to tick.'

'That's one way of looking at it. I'm trying to look at other ways to move the dial in my organisation. One woman in my team has been driving an initiative on building psychological safety in teams. She keeps reminding us that psychological safety is often overlooked when a team is doing well – the 'if it's not broken don't fix it' mentality. But unless we check it, the team may not be meeting its potential if not everyone feels valued for their contributions.'

Steve pondered on this point. Does each of his team members feel valued for their contributions? They should feel valued, but, actually, he realised he's never asked the question. Is he really so removed from the day-to-day? His door is always open, he has told them that…

'OK,' Steve said. 'I need a minute to think about this. It looks like we've got a few things on the agenda to cover today. 1. Something about behaviours. 2. Something about, I don't know, are women being themselves? And 3. Something about being valued for contributions?'

'Psychological safety? It should underpin how the team behaves with each other.'

'Great. Now, where can I get a coffee? We have a lot to work through today and I know I need the caffeine!'

Chapter 1

Acknowledging disrespect in the workplace

People perform well at work when they feel respected and valued. Unfortunately, women in STEM frequently experience disrespect in the workplace, often in ways that are not well understood by their organisation. Disrespect can be both obvious and subtle, and can be harmful when it happens repeatedly. Often what is worse for those impacted is when disrespectful situations are highlighted but no action is taken. These situations need to be acknowledged as well as recognised by organisations in order for actions to be taken to improve their employees' experiences.

During their coffee break, Markus told Steve about the time he had spent after the end-of-year holidays speaking with women in STEM in his organisation. He started with those who take part in the ERG and then looked to make new connections with others to get to know them and to understand their experiences. Steve thought this was a good idea. His organisation didn't have an employee resource group – maybe he could create one?

***

'Steve, I want to share some insights that some women within my organisation have shared with me. I spent a lot of time listening to them. I would love to be able to fix the issues, but the problems are quite complex.'

'Well, let's start there, Markus, and see where we get to before we break for lunch.'

Markus looked through his notes.

'OK, let's start with what I heard from the ERG conversations. They ran a survey across the organisation last year and apparently 65% of women said they experienced sexism in everyday meetings. I was shocked at how high that percentage was. And they say CEOs and directors just don't see the issues.'

'What kind of sexism? Catcalling?' Steve asked in disbelief.

'No, that didn't come up, at least not in offices. Whenever women talked about their on-site experiences, however, catcalling was quite a regular thing that happened.'

'And what did they do when it happened?'

'Nothing, most of the time. They pretended nothing happened and continued on.'

'Well, if they don't report these things, how do they expect it to stop?'

'There were a few stories that came up from women both within my organisation and some external.'

Markus handed a sheet of paper over to Steve to read:

Story 1: 'My inline supervisor told me to invite a supplier out for a drink and wear a low-cut top so he'll remember me. Despite me reporting it to HR, that supervisor is now my line manager.'

Story 2: 'I worked closely with a male colleague where I was the project manager and he was the business analyst. In every meeting or event we went to, everyone would address him and not me – it was like I didn't exist. Also, we both had a PhD. His payslip was addressed to "Dr", but mine was addressed to "Mrs".'

Story 3: 'I was told, "You work a lot of hours, how are you supposed to find a husband if you are working all the time?" and "It's OK if you make that decision because if they fire you, you have a man to take care of you", which wasn't the case. They said these comments to my face.'

Story 4: 'I received pretty bad backlash when I spoke up about emails addressed to "Gents" when they went to me and other women.'

Story 5: 'I was interrupted four times in a 30-minute meeting yesterday, all by the same man. I finally asked if he could please let me finish, and if looks could kill… he told me afterwards that he did not appreciate me speaking to him in such a manner especially in front of others.'

Story 6: 'When I returned from maternity leave, I felt isolated and uncertain on my next role. I needed help and sent a meeting request to a senior manager to explore career options. My current manager was informed and instructed me to retract the meeting request as I shouldn't go over people's heads.'

Steve didn't know what to say. He reread the stories and thought about how he had never heard anything like this from the women within his organisation. Maybe his organisation's culture was just better?

'It was uncomfortable reading for me, too,' Markus said. 'When I heard these stories, I was shocked. I couldn't imagine this happening, but the more I thought about it… I know these stories aren't made up.'

Steve pondered for a moment and then said, 'Could these be isolated events with individuals who just need some coaching?'

'Well, these stories specifically come from women both inside and outside my organisation. But what they're telling us is there is a pattern of behaviours that seem common in more traditional industries, where the men outnumber the women. I started sharing these stories with other women in my own organisation and I didn't find any women that were surprised by them. However, when I shared them with my male colleagues, there was surprise each time. What does that tell you?'

'There's definitely some sort of gap of understanding here. Or women aren't sharing their stories?'

'Maybe it's the men that don't listen?'

Steve shifted uncomfortably. He always felt that he was open to feedback and that it wasn't his problem if women don't want to share issues with him. Why would it be his problem…?

'Look, if a woman comes to me whining about feeling left out, what can I do about that? If I start criticising every man for some off-the-cuff comment they make, I'm going to find myself without any employees at all!'

'I did find a few solutions out there, though, that some organisations have found helpful,' Markus suggested. 'I found a consultant, a man called Tom, who works with male executives on how to achieve gender equity in their organisation.'

'Equity? Not equality?'

'Definitely equity. I learned that equality is like everyone having a pair of gloves, but equity is everyone having a pair of gloves that fit them.'

'Ah… that makes sense. So gender equity is addressing that men and women have different needs?' asked Steve, and as he did, he thought about Markus's earlier comment about alpha males and alpha females and how they can be perceived differently for doing the same thing. 'Actually, never mind, I've got it.'

'Tom explained how many male executives he speaks with struggle to understand the issues as those things have never happened to them.'

'And what did he suggest?'

'He said he encourages them to take a good look at what needs to change in their organisation, why it needs to change, and why they as individuals need to push the change. He says, "Until you ask other people what's happened to them and you're actually interested in what's happened to them, you're not going to find out unless they volunteer it".

'I still don't understand why women wouldn't just share these stories though. If you encourage people to speak up when there's a problem, why wouldn't they just do it?'

'They feel isolated. The women in our ERG said that was the only forum in which they felt comfortable to share their experiences. And that it was difficult to find others who really want to help and support them. The other aspect Tom spoke about was male allies.'

'Male allies? As in, male supporters? But women should have support from their management if they're doing a good job, shouldn't they?'

'I would hope so, but I know I haven't always got on well with my managers,' Markus admitted.

'Yes, that's true!'

After a moment, Steve got up and looked out the window thinking to himself. He checked his watch and saw there was still a bit of time before lunch.

Steve sighed. 'Markus – I'm not sure how we can expect the men in the organisation to get these stories out of the women if the women don't want to share them. I hear regularly how it's so difficult dealing with women today after that 'me-too' thing. You can't put a foot wrong or make any jokes. One team leader of mine says he won't be in an empty room with a woman anymore in case any accusations come his way!'

'I don't think it's a woman's issue or a man's issue, I think it has more to do with how people work with each other. It's about the culture we want in our organisations. I do have some other examples of best practices I've found, if you're interested.'

'Sure, go ahead.'

Markus then shared a conversation he had with Leyla in January. Leyla is on the committee for their organisation's gender-focused ERG and has been involved in their initiatives for three years. She is also an engineer who leads a small team to build and test equipment. Markus invited Leyla to have an open, but confidential, discussion on her observations on the ERG as well as her experiences in the organisation.

***

'It's great to have this conversation with you, Markus. There aren't a lot of men interested in this topic.'

'Yes, that's something I'd like to help with. Tell me about the ERG – what kind of things are you doing?'

'Well, one thing we started doing this year was holding lunch-and-learns on experiences in the workplace. It is hosted by our ERG, but the invites go to everyone. Now, not everyone attends, far from it, but those that do – and I'm meaning the men – get a lot out of it. They hear stories first-hand, and the discussion always continues right up to the end of the time slot. And of course, it's a "what's said on this call stays here" scenario to protect those who choose to share their experiences.'

'And this happens over a lunchtime? How often?'

'Yes. We do them once a month. The team comes up with a topic for discussion and those who are comfortable share their experiences. There are some that join virtually if they can't be in the room, and we make use of the meeting chat.'

'And have you seen a lot of impact from these sessions?'

'We found that many men who attend these sessions for the first time come to future sessions and encourage others to join them,' Leyla replied. 'It's starting to build this community of openness and empathy, where those sharing are in a safe space and are supported.'

'That's great! It's important for people to feel supported. Does this carry over into your day-to-day work?'

Leyla paused and then said, 'Sometimes it does. A few of the men have started calling it out when they see noninclusive behaviours in meetings.'

'What kind of behaviours?'

'For example, if a woman is interrupted or making sure women have a seat around the table rather than perching in the back. It actually happened to me last week where I suggested an idea, the discussion continued, and later a man shared the same idea and this time it was met with praise.'

Markus frowned. 'I'm sorry to hear that. Did someone notice and say something?'

'Well, of course I noticed, but so did one of my male stakeholders who pointed it out. After the meeting some of my female colleagues were talking about it and used the word "he-peat" instead of "repeat" to explain the situation as it happens so often.'

'"He-peat"? I haven't heard that one before,' said Markus, visibly surprised. 'I'm sorry this happened to you, Leyla. It makes me angry if it's happening very frequently. I'm going to make sure I call it out if it happens in front of me.'

'Thanks, Markus. I know many of us will appreciate your support.'

'Not a problem at all. So back to these lunch-and-learns. Has there ever been negative feedback about them?'

'About the session itself? No, none that I'm aware of. Once we had a senior male suggesting we need to stop discussions on gender equity as he felt they weren't needed anymore.'

Markus raised his eyebrows.

Leyla continued, 'So I asked him to come to a session, listen to the experiences shared, and then come back to me and say if he still believes the focus is no longer required. It's really simple – just listening for half an hour. If he still doesn't believe a problem exists after hearing those stories, then he wasn't open to it anyway.'

'So what would you suggest in that situation?'

'Don't fight a losing battle. I know we're not going to fix everything for everyone, but there are wins as well as losses. I encourage the committee to focus on where we can make a positive impact and not to lose sleep or spend too much energy on initiatives and people where it's clear they won't give us what we need.'

'That's healthy.'

***

After relaying the discussion to Steve, Markus added, 'I thought about her final comment about not fighting a losing battle, and people who won't change. I don't know the answer to that one yet. It isn't mandatory to think the same about gender equity, therefore it isn't something we can enforce.'

'This is the problem. How do you fix something that you can't control?' Steve asked rhetorically. 'The repetition in meetings doesn't sound very efficient if ideas need to be repeated to be heard.'

'I think the ERG is doing a great job in bringing some of these issues to the surface. The lunch-and-learns seem to be working great especially as they can be hybrid with some in the room and others dialling in. Speaking of – online meetings could also be a partial solution for your team member, Steve, if he doesn't feel comfortable being alone in a room with a female colleague.'

'I'll be sure to pass that on.'

After further consideration, Markus said, 'But thinking back to gender equity and how people in the organisation feel about it. There are clearly differences in perceptions, whether that's team manager to team member, team member to team manager, or peer to peer. Bias is another element that comes up regularly in discussions.'

'Bias? But I'm not biased.'

'I'm afraid you are, Steve – everyone is. Everyone has biases based on how they've grown up, their experiences, how they've been treated, their relationships, and so on. The problem comes when someone isn't aware of their biases and it impacts how they make decisions – it's unconscious bias that needs to be well understood.'

'Oh wait, I've heard of that. HR has a 2-hour training course on unconscious bias that they launched last year. I don't think it was very popular though.'

'Did it have management support behind it?'

Steve shifted uncomfortably. 'It probably could have been supported better. I only heard of it quite late on when I heard feedback during one of my leadership team meetings. It probably needed to be communicated better.' As Steve said this, he wondered if there had been any emails or meetings he had missed on the topic.

Steve said, 'How about before our next meeting I do some fact-finding on this unconscious bias course and I feed back next time?'

'That sounds good. Well, looks like it's time for lunch, let's go to the canteen.'

***

A number of actions can be taken by organisations and by women when it comes to acknowledging disrespect in the workplace – here are some top tips:

Top Tips for Organisations:

- ⚜ Create an inclusive ERG led by employees with senior-level sponsorship. This will help identify behaviours in the workplace by sharing real-life experiences and ideas of employees without alienating anyone.
- ⚜ Encourage leaders to make time to get to know their people and learn about their experiences directly.
- ⚜ Build a supportive network of men within the organisation to drive behavioural change and highlight the role that they can play.

Top Tips for Women:

- ✪ Ensure disrespectful behaviours are reported using your HR tools and processes and/or reported through your manager or mentor.
- ✪ Take part in ERGs to share your stories and learn how others have handled their respective situations.
- ✪ Highlight if someone repeats your idea in a meeting without acknowledging you. Example: 'Thank you for supporting my idea, which I raised a few minutes ago. What can we do to move it forward?'

Chapter 2

Inauthenticity holds people back

It is very common to find someone in your workplace who doesn't seem authentic. It could be someone who is trying too hard, someone who is mirroring someone else's behaviours, or someone who hasn't quite figured out who they are and who they want to be. While it can bring uncertainty to a team, it can also set a tone of what is and is not acceptable when that individual is a leader. When looking to leaders, junior employees will observe their behaviours and often use them as a guide for reaching a leadership position themselves. However, if adopting those behaviours is inauthentic, the junior employee will lose credibility and struggle to progress, particularly if they are already different.

After lunch, Steve and Markus returned to the meeting room.

***

'You have great lunch options here, Markus.'

'Yes, it's not always so good for the waistline though!'

'Right, we've covered behaviours, what's next?'

'We had two more items on the agenda – the next one is about women being themselves at work.'

'Yes, that's a good one. I have a few initial thoughts if I may?' asked Steve.

Markus nodded.

Steve wanted to make an effort and show Markus that he was engaged in this topic. 'I have seen a few women in my time where they seem to prefer to act like men. You know, the ones who "wear the trousers". Now, I'm all for equal rights and women choosing to work. But I don't know if they're trying to be something they're not or if that's what they're really like. They can be quite difficult to work with.'

Markus felt uncomfortable. 'I don't know if we should say "wears the trousers" anymore, Steve, but I do know what you mean, and some of the women I spoke with mentioned a similar point. The gist of it is that they felt women who act like men are more likely to succeed.'

Steve was puzzled. 'What do they mean "act like men"?'

Markus told Steve about two women who work outside of his organisation, Jo and Sarah. Both are engineers and connected with Markus through a networking event for gender equity in energy.

***

During one of the breaks, Markus asked Jo and Sarah what the working environment is at their workplaces.

Jo said, 'There is very much a blokey type of culture and I think that manifests in a lot of organisations. It does make it harder to fit in when you're the only one who's different.'

'Do you find that impacts your work?'

'Absolutely it does! If I am in a meeting or working on something and need to ask a colleague for clarification, I often wonder if they are judging me for not knowing everything.'

'And how about you, Sarah – have you had a similar experience?'

'Well, even from early in my career, I had times where I was talked over and felt overlooked. I then felt I needed to change my personality and to overwork to be seen – and it worked, but it wasn't right. I felt like I was trying too hard every day, and it didn't feel natural. I think you see this kind of thing more the higher up you look in an organisation.'

'What do you mean? Do you think senior women feel a need to change themselves to fit in, even at their level?'

'Yes, I do think that happens,' Sarah replied. 'I think they have the same issue with the same behaviours, it's just at a more senior level. There's this need to fit in – whether that is through how they dress, how they speak, or even their hair-style. I was told once, by another woman I might add, that to be taken seriously, I need to cut my hair very short as it looks more professional.'

'I wish you were joking. I don't think I've ever been told to cut my hair at work.'

Jo added, 'I've seen lots of those kind of sentiments from senior women also to those more junior – it's like they think their path is the only path and therefore every woman coming behind them needs to do the same thing. It doesn't exactly scream diversity, does it?!'

'No, not at all, but following the paths of others does sound familiar. I've seen some male leaders like that too

– they have a predefined path to success in their minds. But I think the world has moved on and now different people can have different experiences and still be successful. There's definitely much more work for organisations to do to engage and enable women particularly in STEM roles.'

***

After Markus finished conveying the conversation, Steve asked, 'If I understand this correctly, we're saying women feel they have to change themselves to fit in with the culture of the organisation?'

'Fit in as well as progress, but they are recognising it isn't right for both themselves and the organisation. The courses they attend, for example, speak a lot about being assertive, and how to speak so men will listen, but is it really the women that need to change?'

'It depends on the woman, doesn't it? If they have the right skills to be effective at their jobs then no, but if they don't, then yes, the same as anyone else.'

Markus thought for a moment. He imagined a team where everyone looked the same, wore the same clothes, and spoke the same way. It wasn't a team he wanted to be on. But why did he feel that way?

'Steve – I think if everyone in a team, men as well as women, behave the same way, wouldn't the team fall into a rhythm where they do the same thing over and over? I think they would lose all innovation and creativity, and any new person would need to conform or be left out. I don't think that's an environment I would want to encourage.'

'Oh yes, I agree, Markus. Innovation and creativity are critical for any successful business. We don't want to erode that. So what are we saying?'

'We're saying we need to find a way for women, or anyone really, to be accepted even if they are quiet or more reserved, have a different background, or any other reason for being different. And maybe more than that – I think we're saying leadership is evolving?'

'Evolution? That's quite a deep topic!'

'Well, I do think leadership is changing. Back to the alpha male conversation – nowadays we're moving away from command-and-control, and instead wanting teams to solve their own problems without being told. And we also want to encourage diverse thinking – respectful debates, out-of-the-box ideas – we want to promote that.'

'I agree, and those new ideas will be great for the business. One of my direct reports is always going out of his way to include all his team members. He's frequently sharing their ideas with me and talking about how great the team is working. They are doing a great job.'

'That's good, Steve. How does he do it?'

'Well, I'm not sure, I haven't attended any of his meetings with his team. Naturally – I don't want to undermine him – and you know, if it's not broken don't fix it, right?'

'I hope he's not like one guy I used to work with. His name was James and he wasn't who he was trying to be. James was always front and centre when a senior leader was in the room. He was the guy who always asked a question when in a large crowd after a presentation. The spotlight was always on him. I would hear James repeating catchphrases of senior leaders, even though it sounded really inauthentic coming from him.'

'But you want people like James in the organisation to share messages.'

'If he's sharing messages from leadership to his team, then yes, but often James wouldn't share accurate messages upwards – especially when things weren't going well.'

'Well, that's a problem.'

'Yes, absolutely. What made things worse was when things weren't going well, the mask he was wearing would slip and he'd become a different person. Probably his true self. James did well in the organisation until we started implementing 360-degree feedback forms where he had to request feedback from his team. Only then did the leadership start becoming aware of his true behaviours.'

Steve thought about this, then said, 'But what does this have to do with women being themselves?'

'There are too many "Jameses" in the industry. And because they rise high in organisations by being someone they aren't, those who are different – the women – feel even more out of place. One woman I spoke with worked for a "James" of her own and whenever she raised any concerns, "James" would dismiss it. He didn't want any negative press getting to his manager. And the more he dismissed the woman's ideas and opinions, the more she withdrew, until she eventually had only administrative work to contribute to the team.'

'But was that a woman in STEM?'

'Yes, she was,' Markus replied. 'Soon no one in the team recognised her skills for anything other than admin. She eventually left the company because she said she wanted more than just meeting the diversity quota.'

'So the person who thinks differently and challenges the status quo eventually leaves?'

'It seems to be a common occurrence.'

'But organisations are doing something about it?'

'It doesn't seem to be easily recognised by senior leaders, and not by team members early in their career either. You have an experienced person offering to support others by sharing their knowledge, and of course to junior personnel, male or female, this is welcomed. However, it seems that once that less experienced team member shows signs of becoming competition, they become a threat and must be discredited or moved aside to prevent any attention being diverted from "James". For senior management, if they have an experienced employee providing positive reports, echoing their values publicly, and identifying junior employees who need a little extra help, they have no reason not to support them.'

'This can't be only men, though, doing this?'

'I found a few examples of men doing it, at both junior and senior levels of the organisation, but I can see scenarios where a woman could do the same,' Markus replied. 'Squash any threat or any disruption in the team. Like a queen bee.'

'Or king… something…'

Markus laughed. 'If inauthenticity is accepted as the path to success, then organisations risk losing their credibility both internally with their workforce and externally with customers and shareholders. Therefore, inauthenticity can have a real impact on business success from both a reputation and a financial perspective.'

'We need to capture this. Now I'm starting to wonder if my direct report is being authentic or not. I will ask some questions next time we meet. Perhaps questions where he can back up his statements about how great everything is.'

'Let me know how that goes,' said Markus in a light-hearted tone.

Steve took some notes while Markus looked through the material he had assembled in advance of today's meeting.

'So that woman in STEM you mentioned, the one who left the company, is that why a lot of them are leaving?'

'I think it's one of the big reasons,' Markus replied. 'I know some try to combat this by emphasising their qualifications or experience at every opportunity – and you can imagine how well that goes down.'

'Oh, yes, I've seen that, actually from both men and women. A sign of insecurity?'

'Or maybe they can't think of a better way to make sure people know their value. It would be beneficial if women in that kind of situation had someone to talk to – a mentor perhaps to help them navigate the situation. It would also give them an outlet.'

'Yes, agreed,' said Steve.

Markus added, 'Another example of differences in approach is from Abby – she is a woman in STEM within my organisation but in a different department.'

Markus then shared a small part of his discussion with Abby.

***

'Abby – what do you find most frustrating about working in your team?'

Abby thought for a moment and then said, 'What I find most frustrating is when people don't respond or show up when I send meeting requests. What is even worse is when I see them showing up for a meeting when it is called by a man.'

'What kind of meetings are they?'

'For example, stakeholder review meetings or sprint reviews. I was finding it very difficult to get the right people in the room, no matter how often I raised the issue.'

'And what did you do?'

'Well, I had been discussing it with my partner who works for another company. As an experiment, I asked him to write the emails for me and they were borderline rude – no "please" or "thank you". Guess what? People showed up. So I'm left thinking, was I just not being firm enough? It just makes me feel ineffective – like a square peg in a round hole – and to be effective, I need to be like someone else.'

***

Steve listened as Markus shared this story.

'I hear that and think, well, yes, she obviously wasn't being firm enough and her partner has shown her how to communicate more effectively. Wouldn't you agree?'

'Women can have a different style when it comes to communication as we talked about earlier. Much more indirect, but if that's not recognised or acknowledged then there is a gap that needs to be closed to make the communication more effective – on both sides,' Markus added. 'It's another aspect of how women can be different and excluded on that basis.'

Steve nodded and continued his notes.

'We've talked a lot about people being inauthentic as you put it, but if that culture is embedded in an organisation, what can be done?'

'Tom, the consultant I met with, spoke about leading with emotional intelligence and that most of the issues of today require much more rounded thinking than would have been typical in the past. So things like collaboration, showing empathy, showing you care for employees – these are all very important if we want to retain people.'

'So more of the touchy-feely stuff?! But seriously, I can see how this would help keep women in the organisation. It reminds me of my wife and how she would tell me she'd often feel left out when she would accompany me to work events. She said we would either talk about work or football, and she couldn't join in on either topic. Now I try to make an effort to ask my colleagues about their social lives and to find topics they are happy to speak about.'

'That's another good idea, Steve – and it can help teams make connections that they may not immediately identify. It's definitely something these virtual meetings don't help.'

'Yes, I've been saying the same. No more chat before and after the meeting asking how someone is, how their weekend was, how their golf game went! You do miss the people connection.'

'And with that connection you get to know people, build trust, create an affinity with them, and understand their experience and skills as well as their aspirations.'

'You mentioned earlier about queen bees and the Jameses of the world, and we both know people like that, but do we have any examples of what an organisation can do to encourage everyone to be themselves?'

'Role models,' Markus replied. 'Those with genuinely great behaviours need to be held up as role models for others to learn from. Something like "Behaviour Ambassador of the Month or Quarter". Perhaps people could be nominated by their peers or direct reports, so it is a bottom-up approach.'

'I like that idea and it can also include recognising their work and any internal or external recognitions or awards. This will help ensure everyone knows it's about the full package – not just behaviours or performance in isolation.'

'Yes, absolutely!'

'And it isn't difficult to implement either. Yes, this is definitely going on the list.'

'Looks like it's time for a coffee!'

***

Markus and Steve have identified a few issues where both men and women have shown signs of inauthenticity at work that can impact the experiences of women. In Markus's story about James, it is clear that James is not his authentic self at work. Organisational cultures can drive these behaviours especially when someone is recognised and rewarded. Markus's suggestion of 360-degree feedback from direct reports, as well as peers, and senior managers can be very helpful to determine if a person behaves authentically in front of varied audiences.

Another aspect they covered was how some women react when they feel overlooked. They want to become visible and do this by stating their skills or experience. While this can be effective in some instances, like in an introductory conversation with a mentor, it can have negative consequences when done in the wrong situation. The individual may inadvertently create more of a barrier between themselves and their team by appearing arrogant. The right approach in this instance is a judgement call based on the personalities of the team. One neutral option is for all team members to list their skills in a matrix and to identify strengths as well as development areas. This way each team member can identify who has skills in an area where they wish to develop and can partner with them for training. This approach provides value for all members of the team.

Research studies have shown that highly competent women are becoming more confident in leaving an organisation where they don't feel valued and often set up their own business instead. They clearly are motivated, have drive and capability, but were not offered the right opportunities at their workplace to excel.

Markus highlighted several real-life examples of poor behaviours, but through their discussions, Markus and Steve have come up with some good actions that can be taken as shown below.

Top Tips for Organisations:

- ⚔ Lead with emotional intelligence and enable connections to be made across the organisation for team members to get to know each other and build trust.

✦ Be on the lookout for inauthentic people in leadership roles – verify what they tell you.

✦ Identify and showcase suitable role models in the organisation based on their performance, behaviours, and internal or external recognitions.

Top Tips for Women:

✦ Identify a suitable mentor or suite of mentors to help you navigate through challenging situations.

✦ Avoid proving yourself to those around you by regularly referencing your qualifications and experience. You are in your role because you have the capability.

✦ Make space to create real connections with your colleagues to build trust.

Chapter 3

Promoting psychological safety to unlock inclusion

Psychological safety is critical for any individual to feel part of a team. Physical safety has been measured for some time through key performance indicators to understand when someone has been hurt physically. However, psychological safety in some ways has still to be well understood to ensure people are not getting hurt psychologically at work. This can take many forms – for example, exclusion from a group, being held to different standards than others in the team, and microaggressions. Studies have shown women in STEM frequently report a lack of psychological safety at work, which can lead to attrition.

***

'I felt quite uncomfortable at that awards ceremony last year, particularly when they shared the results of those surveys. It was difficult not to feel like I wasn't doing enough to help the situation,' Markus said after they returned from their coffee break.

'I know what you mean,' Steve replied. 'There were certainly some sobering statistics. And that's why we agreed to meet, isn't it?'

'Yes, of course! I'm already seeing clear actions we can take – a lot of which we've covered today.'

'Yes, let's recap. We've covered the type of disrespectful behaviours women experience in the workplace, and then we covered why authenticity is so important both for women and for their leaders.'

'But if we ask them to be their authentic selves and they're treated with disrespect, that won't work. They talk about feeling like a fraud and anxiety and confidence issues, which is awful, and no one should have to go through that.'

'No, and I expect asking them to toughen up isn't the answer either,' Steve said jokingly.

'No, but creating a safe workplace from a psychological sense would be better for everyone. Psychological safety is a big topic and one that doesn't seem well understood across industries.'

'That's not a term I'm familiar with.'

'I had a look online and found a list of seven questions to test your team's psychological safety – it gives a good idea of what it's about. Some of the big names in global companies use it, therefore, it could be a good starting point.'

'Sure, let's see what they say.'

'Here is the list of questions (Braiden, 2020).'

1. If you make a mistake on your team, is it held against you?
2. Are you able to bring up problems and tough issues?

3. Do people on the team sometimes reject others for being different?
4. Is it safe to take a risk?
5. Is it difficult to ask other team members for help?
6. Do people on the team deliberately act to undermine your efforts?
7. Are your unique skills and talents valued and utilised?

'Those seem straightforward,' Steve replied. 'How is this done? Is it through a survey?'

'Some organisations do it as a live poll during a department-wide meeting. All anonymous, of course, but it gives the leadership team a sense of what level of psychological safety exists. Once they have the data, they can act on it.'

'Yes, data is key. Otherwise it's "he-said-she-said". Looking through the questions, they seem applicable across industries. I can take these and ask my leadership team.'

'You may want a cross-section, Steve. Sometimes, as you mentioned earlier, people at certain levels like to make sure they give the "right" answer – not necessarily the accurate one.'

'Oh yes, that's a good point, Markus. Yes, I would need to ensure we can get more involved at all levels.'

'The only question that threw me when I read it was the one about being safe to take a risk. Because in my line of work, we work to remove, avoid, or minimise risks.'

'But what is the intent behind the question? If someone takes a risk, then a psychologically safe workplace would support them, I suppose? If that is the case, perhaps it is because they are trying something new?'

'Yes, I think that's it. It could be "Is it safe to try something new?" instead. That would indicate if the team is supportive of the individual regardless of the outcome.'

'Yes, I agree that could be alternative wording.'

'OK, good. Now, I have some examples of a lack of psychological safety in the team to give us some context.'

'Yes, that would be helpful.'

'I spoke with one woman who leads an on-site team delivering equipment. Her name is Suzy.'

***

'Tell me about your experiences working on-site.'

'Well, it has certainly been eventful,' Suzy replied. 'I can be based at different sites, as I am accountable for work from different equipment suppliers. Some sites are better than others.'

'In what way?'

'Some have good facilities and some, well, let's just say there is room for improvement. At one site we have a client office where I sit with some others from my organisation from a stakeholder team. We've worked together for almost two years, but the relationship has had some ups and downs. I am the only female on-site from my organisation, and I had to ask which of the two toilets I could use, as there were no signs on the doors. I was then told which of the toilets had been assigned to females and which to males. One day one of the site reps from the stakeholder team asked me: "Can we use your toilet when we need to do something smelly as it is further away from everyone else?"'

'He said what?! What did you say?'

'I didn't want to cause a fuss, and as I wasn't there all the time, I didn't think it was too much of an issue… To be honest, I tried not to be there long enough to need to use the toilet.'

'I don't know what to say – that sounds like basic necessities were missing, or just not as they should be.'

'It was similar to when I first went offshore. They said it was a medical issue that there weren't any toilets I could use and eventually decided that I would have to use the cleaner's toilet up by the helideck – which was the opposite end of the platform from where I was working.'

'It definitely sounds like this industry isn't as advanced as I thought we were. So back to your on-site experiences. Other than toilets, how have your experiences been?'

'The stakeholder team and I did have a situation… It started off when the equipment supplier manager told me some of the stakeholder team had been drunk on-site. Of course, I knew this is against company policies and despite the friction between me and the team, I raised it with my manager. He emailed their manager, who then forwarded the email to his team! It resulted in multiple reply-to-all responses swearing about me and my team. On HR investigation, many reply-to-all emails were found, over a long time frame, discussing my incompetence among other disrespectful comments. All within a team of men I was working with for almost two years.'

'I don't know what to say. I'm sorry you had to experience that.'

'It wasn't fun finding out I had been sitting with these guys who had been writing all kinds of things to each other without my knowledge. I was quite upset when I first found out, but after the investigation quite a few people were changed out and the stakeholder team got a new manager who was great.'

'Well, that's good that you got support from the company. But still not good that you had to experience this in the first place.'

***

'That is poor behaviour. I don't know what kind of manager would forward that to their team, on the company email system no less, and encourage more of the same behaviours from their team. That would be incredibly uncomfortable for the woman working with them.'

'I agree,' Markus replied. 'Even if the team weren't saying anything directly to her, there would have been regular microaggressions grinding her down, second-guessing of her decisions, and it wouldn't surprise me if they would have talked over her in meetings.'

'There should have been some management support available to her to step in if needed.'

'I suppose it depends on whether her management spotted the issue, whether she raised it to them, whether they made time to intervene, and so on.'

'Yes, if she didn't highlight the issue, her management may not have known otherwise, but they need to know what is going on with their team members.'

'Only if they are "people people", leading with emotional intelligence as we discussed earlier. Otherwise they may be oblivious to the whole thing.'

'But if they attended those lunch-and-learns hosted by the ERG, they would know what to look out for?' Steve probed.

'Yes, I think so. But there are other ways to help people feel comfortable about opening up. For example, if I want my team to open up with me, or if we are talking about a particularly sensitive topic, I take an approach where I'll talk about something that makes me vulnerable – if I've made a mistake somewhere or asking for help to understand something.'

'And they still respect you afterwards?'

'Yes, Steve. It was difficult at first to be so open because I've always seen leaders having all the answers and being the strength in the team. It was actually a woman in STEM working in IT who gave me the idea after sharing a story with me. Her name is Poppy and we spoke about a month ago. She said she was used to having to prove herself in teams, but there was one manager, a male manager, who had a different approach. He spoke with her in a very transparent and open way, but quietly saying, "We need to meet to discuss the issue. I need your help to understand." And she was more than happy to help him. It was all about being humble and authentic.'

'We mentioned authenticity earlier, too,' Steve replied. 'It seems to be a key attribute for good organisations.'

'Yes, I think it is what makes a big difference from traditional leadership of the past. Another woman I spoke with said how highly she values organisational cultures that are transparent, and how it is very rare. Thinking about transparency and authenticity, it would help to create a much more trusting organisation.'

'I agree with having teams that trust each other, depend on each other, you know who you can count on, but how does this impact women in STEM?'

'A few of the women in STEM I spoke with mentioned not knowing why certain situations played out the way they did. They said they couldn't help but wonder if it was because they were a woman and perhaps it wouldn't have happened if they were a man. The common theme was that if the organisational culture was more transparent and trusting, they would feel more confident in knowing the objective reasons for something occurring.'

'That makes sense,' Steve replied. 'It would stop the women thinking it happened because of who they are rather than it being something they have done.'

'Yes, I think authenticity, transparency, and trust all leads to fairness in the organisation,' Markus added. 'And it would help men, too. There was this young man two to three years out of university, who knew nothing about why we had to install some equipment a certain way. He spent time with an expert – she had about 15 years of experience in this area – but rather than credit her, he passed the knowledge off as his own during his presentations. He didn't even invite her to be in the room. You can imagine how she felt about the whole thing.'

'He was learning. It is only right that he asks for help and learns from others. Though I suppose he should have acknowledged the help he was given.'

'Steve – think of it like this. You have someone come to you for help. You take the time to share your knowledge that you have gained over a number of years. They then pass the knowledge off as their own and get all the recognition for it, and you aren't mentioned at all. Now couple that with being overlooked, disrespected, not valued for your skills – do you see the issue now? It can be a big problem.'

'Oh yes, I didn't mean it like that,' Steve replied, uncomfortably. 'It's a situation you would want to avoid.'

'Yes, without a doubt! When anyone, including women in STEM, adds value to a team, they should be recognised and acknowledged for that value. And we need to make sure no one feels threatened by someone knowing something they don't.'

'Does that happen often?'

'I have seen it a few times, both directly and hearing from others,' Markus replied, quietly. 'And it's not just the men – there are women who are culprits also.'

'Wait, women excluding women?!'

'Yes, it happens more than you'd think. It's the queen bees again – they struggled to get where they are and they do nothing to prevent the struggle of those behind them – like a rite of passage. Other times, they just don't want someone taking the limelight away from them.'

'I see. Back to egos again?'

'Yes, unfortunately, there is often a lot for women to navigate in these organisations. And when the people they work with don't feel psychologically safe, they can lash out. Too often women are told they "only got the job because they are a woman" and it is normally said by a male colleague who probably feels threatened by them. This is the kind of thing that has also come up at the lunch-and-learns.'

'That's concerning. What action is taken when something like this is raised?'

'If it is reported, it is usually condemned, but it is very difficult for organisations to stop all their employees thinking like that, even when they don't say it. Although, thinking about it, one woman said she didn't hear comments like that in her organisation.'

'Is that true? How did they manage that?'

Markus replied, 'She said she thought it was because they have a culture where they keep talking about it. They talk about gender equity, how all their employees feel, asking departments and teams to review their gender balance, and so on. They keep it visible that they aren't where they want to be, but are being transparent about how they intend to get there.'

'And I suppose because they keep everyone involved, no one is alienated?' Steve looked at his watch.

'Yes, I think that is the key. Anything organisations propose needs to be inclusive, otherwise it can become another excuse for poor behaviours from those who don't want to change or don't know why they need to change.'

'This is good stuff. Shall we grab a coffee?'

***

Steve and Markus have covered a lot of ground during this conversation on psychological safety. The experiences shared demonstrate how big an impact the workplace can have on anyone if it is not psychologically safe. Unfortunately, women experience this frequently, and this is one area that organisations need to address as a priority.

Top Tips for Organisations:

- ✠ Run psychological safety polls during department-wide meetings to assess and understand the level of psychological safety understood by your employees.
- ✠ Train all people managers how to build and use emotional intelligence. Encourage leaders to show vulnerability and authentic humility to connect with their teams and build trust.
- ✠ Keep gender equity initiatives visible in the organisation and ensure they are accessible to all.

Top Tips for Women:

- ✠ Raise issues where psychological safety is lacking to your management, a mentor, and/or another senior leader.
- ✠ Speak up when you don't know the answer or you are encountering something new and need help. Identifying gaps in knowledge and asking for help is a strength.
- ✠ Speak up if your work is going unrecognised. Capture your efforts in writing and ensure your line manager has a copy. Share how this work can benefit others in the organisation through internal social media or a town hall.

Summary of part 1

At the end of their first day of reciprocal mentoring, Markus and Steve have each taken a lot of notes based on their discussions. Reciprocal mentoring can be daunting for anyone at any level, but both Steve and Markus are seeing through the commitment they have made to be open to ideas and implement positive change in their respective organisations.

***

'So where have we got to, Markus?' asked Steve when they returned.

'We've covered a lot today. If we look at what we heard last December, I think now we're seeing that the women don't need to be fixed, it is more often the organisational culture that needs to change.'

'And we have a number of ways to start, don't we?'

Markus looked through all his notes taken throughout the day from his conversations with Steve.

'We've covered a lot of things that impact women in organisations like ours: disrespectful behaviours, inauthenticity, and psychological safety. From all our discussions, I see an overriding theme of changing how we perceive women in the workplace.'

'In what way?'

'In the sense that the traditional view of "what men do" – that is, go to work, become experts, be senior leaders – and "what women do" – stay home, raise the children, feed the family – no longer reflects an ever-changing modern society.

But their careers too often suffer due to bias based on that old-school thinking that remains in the system.'

'And this is causing women in STEM to leave the workforce and we're losing that innovative thinking that they bring to teams to solve today's problems.'

'Yes, it's the lack of inclusive cultures, lack of fairness and transparency in the workplace, and often just not feeling valued at work,' Markus replied, 'and yes, they leave.'

'But the solutions we've discussed today, there would need to be a way to get these into the workforce.'

'It only takes one man, someone fairly senior willing to stand up and say this is important. Maybe someone mid-level to senior as you don't want anyone to think they are only doing this for optics. I support this. I champion this.'

'And that is all that is needed?' Steve probed.

'Maybe being vulnerable and perhaps sharing their story of why they think it's so important. And once that starts there could be a domino effect. This is what has happened in other organisations once one person shares a story. One woman told me they often post blogs on their intranet with an option to comment below the blogs and it can start waves of really great discussions.'

'That's another great idea! We have lots of ideas now, and plenty to review between now and our next meeting in June. I'm going to find out more about our unconscious bias course, as discussed earlier. Next time we're focusing more on technical skills and performance, yes?'

'Yes, that's what I have written down. Well, it has been great spending the day on this with you, Steve, and I look forward to our next meeting over in your office in June.'

***

Markus came to this session having done his own research through discussions with women in STEM both internal and external to his organisation. He has very much led the conversation and it is likely due to his intrinsic motivation to support his daughter. Steve, in contrast, does not appear to have done much since the award ceremony in December. He is focused on improving the business, and the link between DEI and business performance can be tenuous at times from Steve's perspective. Nevertheless, Steve has engaged with Markus and has an opportunity to take action before the next meeting. He could be that one senior person to publicly support the gender-equity goals of his organisation and encourage others to do the same.

Markus is learning from Steve. He is seeing first-hand how more traditional managers may interpret reports of poor behaviours, disrespect, and exclusion. There are many leaders who exhibit similar behaviours to Steve's, even in Markus's organisation, but to create real sustainable change these leaders need to be held to account. This starts with them looking in the mirror and understanding themselves, their behaviours, and their biases.

It can be difficult for leaders like Steve to relate to the experiences of women. Their own experiences are often very different. Where men like Steve have typically navigated situations with ease by adopting command-and-control behaviours of previous leaders, women often do not have that option. One approach that Markus is adopting is to listen with curiosity with the intent to understand experiences from their perspective. He is fact-finding and tries hard not to make anyone uncomfortable by judging their feelings or actions. At the same time, Markus is showing empathy to the women he meets with, and leads with emotional intelligence.

Poor behaviours in the workplace can lead to toxic cultures that impact everyone. With the right behaviours where everyone is respected, encouraged to be their authentic selves, and supported every day to perform at their best, organisations will have the potential to motivate employees with improved business performance.

PART 2

INCLUDE THE RIGHT TECHNICAL SKILLS AND RECOGNISE PERFORMANCE

The three months pass and while both Steve and Markus get busier at work, they stay committed to their reciprocal mentoring agreement. Markus continues engaging with his organisation's ERG and meeting with women in STEM to learn about their experiences and identify how he can help. Steve, on the other hand, spends a lot of time with his customers to better understand their requirements and to ensure his organisation is best placed to meet them. He has gained a few big contracts and as such has started a recruitment drive. Steve has made it clear to his team that they need diverse teams to stay competitive and need to recruit with that view in mind. While this has taken most of his attention, Steve has also started speaking with women in STEM in his organisation.

In mid-June they meet again, this time at Steve's office.

***

'Steve! Great to see you again. It's been a busy few months!'

'Yes, it's been a busy time here also. Last time we met, we spent a fair amount of time on behaviours that women in STEM face in the workplace. I wrote down that we are discussing inclusion of technical skills today – is that right?'

'Yes, I had that noted also. It was about making sure women are included for having the right skills to meet the business needs.'

'I took some time last month to meet with some women in STEM within my organisation,' Steve said proudly. 'I took a group to lunch and we had a good discussion about a few topics, but one I particularly focused on was how valued they feel for their technical abilities.'

'What did they say?' Markus probed. 'I'm really curious.'

Steve described the discussion to Markus.

***

'Gabriella, in your introduction you mentioned you have been in the software development team for the last year, is that correct?'

'Yes, that's correct. I was in quality before and then moved into development.'

'And how is it working in the software team?'

'Well, sometimes it can be great, and other times, well, we just get on with it.'

'What do you mean? You can speak freely.'

'Well,' Gabriella replied uncomfortably, 'sometimes I feel like I'm not in the club.'

'The club?'

'The boys' club. You know, they all chat, socialise, have worked together on previous projects.'

Other women in the group nodded with support. Steve was confused.

'And is that important to you?' Steve asked, choosing his words very carefully.

'It does make a difference,' Gabriella replied. 'For example, I feel like I'm working all the time. I have my core project work, and I'm also involved in other company initiatives where we arrange events. As well as that, I spend time mentoring and coaching less experienced colleagues, and then when I go home I have to feed my family, put the kids to bed, check my email in case of any queries from colleagues in other time-zones, and then I can get to bed. But despite all this, I don't think the team sees me.'

'That is a busy day you have.'

As Gabriella spoke, Steve tried to map her experience to his own. When he was at Gabriella's stage in his career, he wasn't involved in any company initiatives – in fact, throughout his career he had sponsored them, but was never the one doing the work. His wife would take care of everything when he got home and he didn't often need to open his laptop again until the next day at work. Steve couldn't see a lot of similarity between his and Gabriella's experiences, and he had always felt that his efforts had been recognised.

'What do you mean by "sees you"?'

'Whenever there's a new initiative in the team or an opportunity to present to senior management, I'm never selected,' Gabriella said, visibly sad. 'I have openly volunteered a few times, but it's always the same guys who are chosen.'

'Have you spoken with your manager about this?'

'He said I just need to be patient. What I've noticed over the past year is that it does get to me after a while. Maybe I need to do more training if they don't think I'm good enough.'

***

Markus sighed when Steve finished telling the story. 'She sounds like she struggles with confidence in her skills.'

'Yes,' Steve replied, 'which is surprising because I spoke with my team about her and she has an exceptional background both academically and professionally. I was quite surprised she feels like that.'

'And when she described her day and everything she does inside and outside work. That's a lot.'

'Yes, and a few of the other girls said their days are very similar. They have a busy home life and a busy work life, but they seem to merge into one with the out-of-hours work they contribute.'

'Do they do this by choice or because it is expected?' Markus probed.

'As an organisation, we haven't specified a requirement to remain available once they go home. I see these girls as really brilliant, but they said they feel that they need to be twice as good, get endorsements from others, and have 101 other things for one of their male peers to consider coming to them for support.'

'Steve – I think you need to stop referring to them as "girls", Markus said sharply. 'It sounds like you're putting them down.'

'Oh really?' Steve asked. 'I never thought of it that way. I always thought women liked to think of themselves as young.'

'Not in the workplace. Anyway, as sad as it is, I heard similar sentiments from women within my organisation, too. I know not all are in the same position. Not everyone has kids at home, not everyone is able to work after they leave the office – virtual or physical – but the aspect about how they feel they are valued for someone to ask them for help seems to be a common issue.'

Steve added, 'One of the other girls, I mean women, Maria, in the digital deployment team, shared another example.

She told me she was working on a project with a group of guys and kept getting information second-hand. They kept calling each other to discuss the work and didn't include her, although it was her area of expertise. Maria eventually realised she was doing significantly more than they were and was very frustrated about it.'

Markus sighed and shook his head.

Steve continued, 'When she shared this with the group, other women shared similar stories. They said if others exclude them, it makes them feel they are not good enough and that makes them strive to do more and more.'

'Imposter syndrome mixed with perfectionism.'

'Yes, exactly, and by doing so they are more likely to suffer a burnout and the business is impacted.'

Markus paused and thought about how he would feel if Isabella felt she wasn't good enough. He had read about imposter syndrome – and how common it is among women in male-dominated work environments – when a person does not believe the successes or opportunities they have achieved are due to their skills and efforts, and instead see themselves as a fraud or imposter in their role. Markus began thinking of the ways he encourages Isabella and how they could translate into the workplace…

'I wonder how often managers recognise it when the women in their team are feeling like imposters. But more importantly, a good way to combat it would be for the managers to recognise the good work and contributions to the team.'

'That sounds good, Markus, but what I'd like to understand is why their teams don't include them in the first place.'

'I've seen some material on this and had feedback from some men. They speak about women's voices being annoying due to their higher pitch and speaking too quickly. You can see some female public figures who deliberately speak lower and slower to get around that.'

'They lower their voices?'

'I know! I was surprised, too,' Markus replied. 'There's also this other thing. I've seen in a few places that apparently men apply for a job when they can meet 60% of the job description, whereas women won't apply unless they meet 100%.'

'Why on earth not? If they don't apply in the first place, they definitely won't get it. Is this why we have so few women in STEM at senior levels?'

'It may contribute to it, but it may also mean we have men in roles where there are women more qualified. But is no one telling the women to apply? I also wonder if male hiring managers assess a woman's application against 100% of the requirements, whereas for a man, there's a bias that he'll be able to figure things out and therefore they'll only assess against, say, 60% of the requirements.'

'Do you think that happens?'

'I don't know, but it wouldn't surprise me,' Markus replied.

'In any case, managers should be providing feedback to the women who report to them to understand where they are and whether they have sufficient capabilities for the advertised role.'

'That would be ideal, I don't know how often it happens in practice though. I have a suspicion that many organisations with women in STEM may have superstars hiding in plain sight.'

'And they could be making a huge difference to the business.'

Markus thought for a while and then said, 'Compared with men, there are a disproportionate number of women doing lower-level work – that is something we can explore. I also think the point about feedback to women is an important one, and also inclusion, in general. How about those for our topics today?'

'That sounds good, Markus. Let's go with them and see where we get to. Now, let me show you the coffee area.'

Chapter 4

'Office housework' crowds out the best work

In many organisations, many women are expected to take on the 'office housework' whether this is part of their core responsibilities or not. This work adds to their workloads and is often not recognised as adding value to the business, especially at annual appraisal time. This can result in women experiencing high frustration from regular assignment of the admin tasks or having to volunteer over a wall of silence to ensure work progresses. It is unclear whether this work is acknowledged and its importance understood by all.

***

'Have you heard of the term "office housework", Steve?' Markus asked while bringing their coffees back to Steve's office.

'What, cleaning the office?'

'No! It's a term that is used to describe work that women typically do like organising team events, taking meeting minutes and issuing actions, identifying meeting times when everyone is available, making the slide deck for someone else's meeting, booking meeting rooms, managing distribution lists – that kind of thing.'

Steve paused and thought about these activities and who normally does them in his team. He couldn't think of a time where it was a man, but it wasn't something he had seen as an issue.

'But if they didn't want to do it, surely they'd say so?'

'People like to be a good citizen, a team player, which means if they're asked to do it, particularly women, they often don't say no. Sometimes the activity is needed and when no one else volunteers, it will most likely be a woman who will step up.'

'But if they have volunteered, then what is the issue?'

'I would say there are a few issues. I spoke with a woman called Dawn recently. She is a lead engineer and shared her experiences with me.'

***

'Oh, I'm regularly tasked with this stuff,' Dawn said about administrative-type activities. 'I end up working over and above my core responsibilities.' As Dawn spoke, Markus could tell this wasn't new – she had been working this way for some time.

'How much of your day does this admin work take up?'

'It's probably about 60% of my day. I mean, it's not consistent, it really depends what is happening. If we are coming up to a big review and we need a slide deck, meeting invites to be sent, a meeting room to be booked, sometimes catering – you know, that kind of thing. Other times, it's for me to write up actions for the team to take and send them to the manager for him to distribute. It does vary.'

Markus paused and thought about what Dawn was saying. He had always been used to booking rooms himself for his meetings and issuing invites directly. It was strange to him that someone would ask someone else in the team to do it when it is more efficient for them to do directly.

'Does anyone else ever take on this kind of work?'

'Sometimes, but mostly the room goes quiet and then I'm asked to do it. I guess it's because I'm female and look younger than others in the room!' Dawn said with a chuckle.

'Do you really think that's why?' Markus probed.

'Honestly, yes, I do, but it's not something I would raise or complain about officially anyway. It's not too bad really, in general, but at the moment there is so much work to do, both my core job and this other stuff, that I feel like I'm very much on a path to burning out.'

'What would happen if you said "no" next time you were asked?'

Dawn seemed uncomfortable with the question. 'I could… but I don't want to be "that person" who thinks they are above doing admin. And I don't want people to think I'm being difficult or not taking one for the team. It's hard enough already to fit in with the rest of the team and I think if I said no, it would give them another reason not to include me.'

***

When Markus finished, Steve said, 'But if that is not her job, she should make sure the person who is accountable for doing that work does it. Don't they have an admin girl?'

'Administrative *assistant*, perhaps,' Markus corrected him sternly. 'But with all the downsizing in the industry lately, lots of those roles have been seen as non-essential as the team themselves can cover the work. And unfortunately, in most cases, the women are the ones who pick up the slack.'

'OK, but most people do work outside of their formal job description. I know we don't want anyone to burn out, but sometimes we just need everyone to pull together and get these things done.'

Steve wasn't sure what the issue was. He thought about his experiences and concluded that he had always had junior female colleagues carry out this kind of work. Was this an issue that he had never realised?

Markus thought for a moment and considered what he had heard through his discussions and seen from his own experiences. He put himself in Dawn's shoes and thought about what he would do and how he would feel in her situation. 'I have another example that may help. This one is from Natasha, a project manager who has an engineering background.'

***

Natasha said, 'I went to a meeting and this person from another company said: "Would you mind taking the minutes? I know you'll do a much better job than all the men." I was the only woman in the room and didn't want to make a scene.'

'So what happened?'

'I just got on with it. I was really mad, but even when I first protested, it was clear I was going to end up doing it.'

'I'm sorry that happened to you, particularly in front of external people.'

'Yes, it definitely felt like I'm going to be stuck with taking minutes all the time with them.'

'Have you ever experienced something like that before or was this a one-off?'

'No, there have been a few times. Another time I was asked to arrange a follow-up meeting with a sales team to onboard them for a new software package that I had worked with for months. I set it up, and two hours before the meeting, I was contacted by both of my senior managers. They asked, "Oh, are you happy to do that meeting? I know it's quite late in the day. I can take it if you want?" I said, "No, it's fine, I've got this." One of them said he'd come along. I went to the meeting and my boss talked and talked, answered every single question and I couldn't get a word in. It turns out they only wanted me to set up the meeting.'

Markus thought through what Natasha said and then replied, 'That's not good, Natasha. That's poor leadership from your managers, both in terms of communication and a complete lack of empowerment.'

'I'm glad you said that, so it's not just me thinking it.'

***

'That doesn't sound very efficient,' Steve said while wondering if Natasha could easily have been a woman in his own organisation. 'Couldn't she have spoken up in the meeting and made herself heard?'

'If the psychological safety doesn't exist between her and her management, I don't think she could have spoken up. It's more frustrating for women when they are treated that way in front of external parties – they won't have the right level of credibility suitable for their actual role.'

'Yes, that could be a problem, I see what you mean. Was there anything else mentioned?'

'The only other comment that came up on this topic was that no one gets credit for this type of work. It isn't recognised in annual appraisals. In fact, a lot of work outside of their core responsibilities doesn't seem to get the appropriate recognition it deserves – this includes things like employee resource group activities and diversity and inclusion initiatives.'

'But as we discussed last time, those are important to the business. Couldn't the women themselves make sure those activities are recognised?'

'Yes, that is something I think they should do if all else fails,' Markus replied. 'Recognition of doing the work is important, but ideally you want to avoid it becoming default that the women in the team are tasked with this stuff.'

'What would you suggest?'

'Well, first off, I would suggest making sure all work is visible. The office housework as well as the "glamour work" – you know, the work that people will get a lot of visibility and praise for doing. You want to make sure team members have a fair share of opportunities for the good stuff and share the load for the administrative work.'

'You'd need to make sure they have the skills and capability for the big jobs,' Steve said, choosing his words cautiously.

'Yes, and you could do that when identifying the work. In fact, you could probably use this as an opportunity for developing team members. They could pair up with a more experienced person who would normally do that work and work together.'

'If there was time and the more experienced team member had the space to do so, then yes, I could see that working.'

'Something like a working agreement would help set the kind of work culture a team wants for themselves. It could drive a great discussion on what would happen if, say, no one books a meeting room, and what they would expect to happen. It can ensure there will be a fair division of responsibilities if done right.'

'I like that idea,' Steve replied. 'It sounds a bit like a team contract.'

'Yes, I've seen them used in a few teams and they work quite well. And we should also ensure teams are recognising *all* good work. Sometimes office housework takes significantly more time than anyone thinks it should, like organising workshops or away days, for example. It takes perseverance to get these tasks completed and that work is all too often overlooked. Not only will this recognition make people feel good, both after completion and volunteering for such work, but it will remove any view that only "superstars" get the glory. And it needs to be authentic – definitely nothing condescending.'

'Once I was in a meeting where a team lead recognised one of his team members in the meeting for setting up a meeting with a client. I thought it was good that he mentioned her, but afterwards I overheard her saying: "He may as well have congratulated me for tying my shoes this morning." I didn't recognise it at the time, but maybe she felt she was only being seen for her office housework skills?'

'Yes, sadly I've heard that kind of thing before also. It sounds like she was feeling undervalued, and getting praise for setting up a meeting probably wasn't the recognition she was looking for.'

'What would you do in that situation?' Steve probed.

'It's difficult without knowing the individual or the team. In general, I think we need to be mindful that some people have a lot of bias – conscious or unconscious – and may still be of the view that admin gets done by women or the most junior person in the team. The other issue, as we mentioned earlier, is if the same woman is always doing the office house-work on top of the job she was hired to do, she is probably working more than her normal hours. And it probably isn't one-off either; it is probably something that happens regu-larly. Imagine spending your main hours in meetings about your core job, and then at lunchtimes or at home that evening spending time on the "thankless tasks".'

Steve stayed quiet and started reflecting.

Markus continued, 'Then they miss all the value women can bring to the team – the diversity of thought that will lead to innovative solutions. You want to tap into all that to generate the best outcomes for the business. And… motivate the women in your organisation. Recognition is a powerful motivator.'

'Yes, agreed. And if we can get the teams to harness the best ideas from all the brains in their team, they will get the best solutions. I like your comment about development opportu-nities, too – that would also serve as a good motivator.'

'Yes – you don't want to hinder anyone under a mountain of thankless tasks, instead you want to be unlocking their potential through activities that stretch them while ensuring they have appropriate support available. Can you just imagine, you have a person in the team with the right solution to an ongoing problem, but you never get to hear it because they are overloaded managing distribution lists and booking meetings?'

'That would be incredibly disappointing if organisations were taking such a risk with their business. Well, it's getting close to lunchtime, how about we head downstairs and beat the rush?'

***

When motivated and ambitious women join an organisation, they want to be challenged and given opportunities for growth. Unfortunately, for too many, they are often the default person asked to do the office housework. This type of unrecognised work neither challenges them nor will it lead to a promotion, yet they are still the ones to do it. After some time, this can leave them disengaged and their image impacted by the rest of the team, leading to them eventually leaving. The longer-term impact can be significant, especially if the women have more office housework than their core responsibilities. It can lead to demotivation and increase imposter syndrome if they feel this is the only work they are trusted to deliver.

There are actions that both organisations and women can take to address this situation, and some are shown below.

If this type of work is more evenly distributed or removed altogether, women in STEM will have more space to focus on their core responsibilities, and will be recognised by their colleagues for the real value they add to the team.

Top Tips for Organisations:

- ✠ Make the office housework activities clearly visible and drive a fair division of tasks, both office housework and glamour work, through a team working agreement.
- ✠ Authentically recognise all good work.
- ✠ Ensure all team members are clear on how their work contributes to the overall business and their leaders are able to articulate it clearly.
- ✠ Verify how women in STEM are seen in the team and, if necessary, advocate for them to be recognised for their technical capabilities.

Top Tips for Women:

- ✠ Ensure all work you do is reflected in your annual appraisal to ensure nothing is invisible.
- ✠ Feel confident in not volunteering to take on office housework activities on behalf of the team if no one else volunteers.
- ✠ Feel confident in saying 'no' if the office housework always comes to you, and advise the requestor of the last time(s) you did it. Also explain that doing this work will take your time away from your core responsibilities.

Chapter 5

Feedback is a gift

Feedback is one of the most important things an employee can get to understand their performance. It should feel real and legitimate, offering value towards real continuous improvement. Whether it is requested or offered, constructive feedback can help identify blind spots and improve effectiveness. However, this is not always how it works in practice.

***

'I've never liked the term "feedback is a gift"', said Steve on their return from lunch.

'Why?' Markus asked, visibly surprised. 'If someone takes the time to provide feedback to help someone improve, is that not a gift?'

'It's the way the term is thrown around these days. Like a cliché.'

'Maybe. Usually it's to encourage people to be receptive to feedback, but I'm not sure if that's always how it feels.'

'Feedback is very important for an employee to know how they are doing at work. But it does need to be delivered in a constructive way. After all, the intent is to help the person improve.'

'In terms of feedback that women in STEM receive, I don't think it's that good. We all want and need feedback that is SMART – you know, Specific, Measurable, Achievable, Relevant, and Time-bound. You want to know what you're good at and where your blind spots are. But what I heard from the women I spoke with was that the feedback they receive is very general.'

'General like "great job!" and that's all?'

'Yes, that kind of thing. The positive feedback tended to be general and not always relevant to where they saw their career going. For example, getting a "well done" for booking a meeting room.'

Steve sighed. 'More office housework.'

'Indeed. Many women mentioned that when they asked for specific feedback on what it would take to move to a more senior role, the responses were equally vague and unhelpful. I spoke with Joy, a project engineer, about this.'

***

'What kind of feedback have you received at work?' Markus asked.

'Often not very helpful,' said Joy. 'Sometimes I ask for feedback from my manager or someone else in the team, but often I just get "great job" as a response. It doesn't help me improve.'

'What kind of feedback would you prefer?'

'I know I'm not perfect. It would be helpful if they could tell me at the time, when I did something wrong or if there was a better way to approach something. That way I would know to do it differently next time or at least understand how my actions were interpreted.'

'That sounds like a good idea – timely feedback. And, yes, it would enable you to immediately make any changes, if needed.'

'Yes, that's exactly what I want.'

'So what is in the way of that?' Markus asked, deliberately probing.

'I think people generally don't like to give feedback where it may upset the person. But I don't think they realise I'm not going to burst into tears! I would love it if someone would tell me things I can improve and provide examples of how to improve. It would improve my skills and will help me be more competitive when applying for my next role.'

'Absolutely! So is there a way you can communicate that with someone when you ask them for feedback?'

Joy thought about this then answered, 'Yes, I could do that. I don't think it would be strange to say it like that either.'

***

'Before we dive into that, I have another example,' Markus said. 'I asked Anita, a team lead in the digital solutions team if she thought the way we give feedback here is effective.'

'And what did she say?'

'She said, honestly, no. She talked about receiving some quite strange feedback in her career. Feedback from various line managers telling her: "You're so noisy", "You're only interested in your own scope", "You don't swear or go drinking with them or follow the football so they don't see you as part of their tribe – maybe you should look for a different role in another team", "You need to be more irreverent", and "If you are interested in people you belong in HR." She had no idea what to change or how to change, which left her in an endless loop and feeling really negative.'

'None of those comments seem particularly helpful for either Joy or Anita,' Steve said, visibly angry. 'How common is it that women are receiving feedback like this?'

'I'm not sure. There is definitely a trend that women are not always getting honest, constructive feedback that they can use to improve.'

'Is it because their managers don't spend enough time with them and don't take the time to gather the right feedback?' Steve asked.

'Possibly. One woman said she hardly ever received feedback from her manager. She didn't get on well with him, but asked for feedback from him anyway. When he did send her feedback over email, he copied in his manager. She was unhappy with what he wrote and said it felt like he was trying to discredit her with a senior leader.'

'Was the feedback inaccurate?'

'I can't say for sure, but what was clear was that it was a surprise. And if the first response is defensive, it doesn't sound like there's a lot of psychological safety there.'

'Yes, that's true. Here we encourage all managers of people to have conversations with their direct reports twice a year – one at annual appraisal time and one mid-year.'

'I think that's a common frequency – we have the same. I hear some companies are trying to encourage continuous conversations to avoid any surprises and make sure both parties are aligned to foster more of a continuous improvement approach.'

'They need to be constructive conversations though.'

'Yes, absolutely,' agreed Markus. 'And both parties need to approach the conversations with a degree of humility – either side could be aware of something the other is not. That reminds me of another woman in STEM who shared this story with me – her name is Michelle. She works in another organisation as a team lead in an operations role.'

***

'You mentioned how your organisation promotes providing continuous feedback. Have you always found that to be effective?'

'I had some feedback from my line manager once,' Michelle replied. 'He said he was told I was disrespectful in a meeting. When I asked for more details, he said he didn't know as he wasn't there and he wasn't told anything else by the man who reported it. That man has never respected me or my role.'

'What happened next?' Markus probed.

'My manager reprimanded me. And I didn't think it was right. The meeting I had attended had over a dozen people present. I spoke with two I knew well who said they did not understand and perhaps they had missed that part.'

'So the man who complained had a different perspective from others who attended the meeting?'

'Either that or he did it deliberately. I then wrote to the meeting chair (a vice president) apologising if my behaviour had been disrespectful and that it was not my intention. He responded saying, "There was nothing disrespectful about your behaviour in that meeting, keep doing what you're doing", and asked the HR manager to investigate the claim.'

'What happened then?'

'Nothing. I never heard anything more, but it was good to know the VP supported me.'

***

'It makes you wonder, doesn't it?' Steve said. 'What was the intention there of the man who complained? It's clear her line manager just followed suit – could that be bias again?'

'It could very well be,' Markus replied. 'It could be political, or it could be a sign of someone feeling threatened by the woman.'

'It does sound like something is going on there. There seems to be an overriding theme where good, constructive feedback is missing. Is there anything we can share with women to help them navigate those type of conversations?'

'There is a *Harvard Business Review* article that describes a Situation-Behaviour-Impact (SBI) approach. I understand it to be like this...'

Situation: When the feedback provider describes the situation, have they understood it the same way as the recipient? If not, this could be an opportunity to add any missing important context. This can include external aspects as well as emotional ones – for example, how the recipient was feeling during the situation prior to any action.

Behaviour: What is it they saw the recipient do (or not do) and is that how the recipient remembers it? Was the recipient's behaviour interpreted in the same way as the recipient intended? Was there any missing context?

Impact: How does the feedback provider see the impact of the recipient's behaviour? Is it from only their perspective or from others' perspectives too? Is it different from how the recipient would see it in their position? Is it how the recipient intended their behaviour to be perceived?

(Davey, 2015)

'Specific examples are the most important aspect of providing feedback – positive or negative – because otherwise it becomes too theoretical and can be debated endlessly,' Steve replied. 'Once both sides can get alignment on what they want compared with what is happening now, they can move forward.'

'Hopefully the recipient sees it that way, too. You'd hope the feedback provider is being honest and supportive.'

'Yes, that's another critical aspect here. That's all about *how* feedback is given and received, but are women getting the right kind of feedback?'

'What do you mean, Steve?'

'Well, I mean, if we want women, particularly those in STEM roles, to reach their potential and to add diverse thinking to the team... Are they getting feedback on their technical skills?'

Markus thought for a moment. Had he heard anything about technical feedback?

'That's a good point, Steve. Anytime I have asked about feedback, the women in STEM I have met with only spoke about feedback on their behaviours. That is a little odd, isn't it? What kind of feedback would your organisation normally provide to an employee?'

'Well, during the end-of-year review, each employee is measured against their objectives for the year – did they meet them, how they behaved while working to reach them, and any general feedback. I suppose if the objectives set at the start were vague, their end-of-year review isn't going to help very much.'

'Does anyone check their objectives?'

'No, it is just between the manager and the junior employee. And to be honest sometimes during the end-of-year review it is just a conversation on how the year has gone – and they don't refer to the objectives at all.'

'And no one notices or picks up on that?'

'No. There's never any reason to intervene.'

'So how does the organisation know if the women, or anyone really, know what to focus on for the next step in their career? If they worked for someone who wasn't supportive of them progressing due to any number of reasons, how would anyone know?'

'I don't know,' Steve admitted quietly. 'We're back to behaviours and organisational culture again on that one.'

Markus thought for a while about what he had seen on career development. There were always training options offered: sometimes people would be told to attend a particular course and sometimes they would request a course. Then Markus remembered something.

'I once saw some career path illustrations of senior leaders. It showed the type of roles they had done that had culminated in their current role. Then anyone looking would have an idea of what to do next to get to where they had.'

'That's a good idea. I haven't seen that before. You would need to know the type of work and type of skills they picked up during each role to make that effective.'

'Yes, that's true. And it may be some of those roles don't exist anymore.' Markus thought some more.

Steve added, 'When you go for professional registration at any of these professional bodies, there are often competences that need to be met – for example, to become a chartered engineer or chartered project professional. It provides a pathway for people to follow to ensure they meet the requirements. Aligning to something like that would assure industry-wide development.'

'That's a great idea. Why reinvent the wheel if there are already tried-and-tested approaches in the industry for recognition of technical skills?!'

'It makes career progression planning very objective as there are certain requirements needed to meet the competences and, ultimately, to gain the professional recognition.'

'Yes, that can help remove any bias from the discussion also. There was one study I read recently that said organisations consistently underestimate the potential of their female employees and that contributes to almost half of the gender promotion gap. The irony is that in the study they found women on average received higher performance ratings.

'So they do the job better, but are less likely to be promoted?' Steve asked, visibly puzzled. 'That doesn't make any sense. Surely those who do the best job should get the promotion?'

'You would think so, wouldn't you? No wonder the gender ratio for women in STEM gets worse the higher you look in an organisation.'

'Feedback is definitely one area we can look at within our respective organisations. There are a number of aspects here that make me wonder if my organisation is guilty of letting down the women in STEM in our organisation. And I want to make some enquiries to understand the current ways of working.'

'I'm in the same place, Steve. Lack of recognition is one sure way of demotivating any employee, including women in STEM, and it doesn't surprise me at all that it results in them leaving organisations. If we want to keep them engaged and retain them, we need to look at how they are receiving feedback. And speaking of feedback, my stomach is craving a snack – time for a coffee break?'

***

Feedback is incredibly important for anyone, including women in STEM, to continue developing at work. Ideally, feedback should be provided to individuals on behavioural, technical, and leadership aspects to ensure they can plan their development activities in a well-rounded manner. Both Steve and Markus are aligned on this and appreciate the importance of their personnel receiving actionable feedback, but recognise there is clearly work to be done in both organisations.

Top Tips for Organisations:

⚜ Ensure managers get to know the members in their team and provide regular feedback to avoid any surprises.

⚜ To mitigate bias, ensure feedback is constructive and SMART (Specific, Measurable, Achievable, Realistic, Time-Bound) and consider use of the Situation-Behaviour-Impact approach.

⚜ Ensure feedback covers the right areas for the desired career progression – this should include technical skills, behavioural skills, and leadership skills. Examples of career paths of senior leaders and competency requirements for professional registration can help.

⚜ Be mindful of bias when potential is assessed. Ensure there is a clear connection to performance to date.

Top Tips for Women:

⚜ Request regular feedback from managers as well as colleagues.

⚜ If feedback is vague, utilise the Situation-Behaviour-Impact approach to draw out specific feedback to address.

⚜ Learn from senior leaders about their career paths that are of interest and look into professional registration requirements to help guide your development needs.

Chapter 6

Bias hinders recruitment, innovation, and growth

Global companies today need to reflect the customers whom they serve. Unfortunately, it is uncommon for this to be the case. In many organisations, employees have similar backgrounds, and the majority will have similar career histories that got them to their current role. This does not lead to diversity in teams.

Organisational leaders can achieve diversity through both internal and external recruitment to represent their customers and bring different perspectives to the team. However, if the new recruits are not included, the value they bring is lost.

On the way back from the coffee area, Steve and Markus reflect on the differences in their respective organisations' coffee areas.

***

'For the last few years, we've had the normal milk and sometimes I see the non-fat variety in there,' said Steve. 'But I don't know if that's because someone brought it in.'

'It's funny when you think about it,' Markus replied. 'Milk being an example of how inclusive a workplace is. We've got dairy milk, but also almond and soy are available. I've also seen lactose-free milk recently, too. Lots of options for people to have their refreshments as they please, and no assumption that everyone will want the same.'

As they returned to Steve's office, Markus said, 'So many of the negative experiences women face in the workplace are driven by bias. And although some organisations have started running unconscious bias training programmes, the research tells us that many of the programmes do nothing, and some even have a negative effect!'

'So after doing training on unconscious bias, people become even more biased?!'

'Unfortunately, so. Some people after training only took the message that biases are unavoidable and widespread, and therefore they could do nothing about it. In other cases, the training was not mandated, which meant those who signed up were the ones who were probably already aware of biases, whereas those who would benefit most were unlikely to attend.'

'That's a difficult one. Mandating the training has advantages, but that action in itself may lead to negative assumptions from employees, not to mention the costs incurred.'

'I don't think it applies to all unconscious bias training, but organisations definitely need to ensure they address it in the right way, and in a way that tracks results over a period of time. Training is important, and organisations need to make sure the training itself is not biased!'

'Biased in what way?' Steve probed.

'Well, for example, one woman I met spoke of a training course she attended where all the required reading was from male authors. When she suggested some books from female authors to balance the list, her HR department ignored the suggestion.'

'That could be bias, but it could also be laziness. But in any case, minimising bias-driven decisions can only be positive for the business. I can think of two areas where bias needs to be well understood – hiring and, of course, during the actual work.'

'I have heard some stories on both of those,' Markus replied. 'One woman I spoke with in the design industry told me about how they recruit their graduates. There was this graduate show each year to which universities would send their top students to showcase their work. Companies would employ from that pool of graduates, but wouldn't look outside.'

'Which means if the university didn't put you forward, you lost your opportunity with those companies also?'

Markus nodded.

Steve replied, 'Again, it sounds like those companies are missing opportunities. And, speaking of bias, if the universities were to be biased in selection, and the companies are biased because they only hire from that show, those that miss out have a double whammy.'

'And it's not just graduate recruitment. When I spoke with Tom, the consultant, about it he told me a story about a hiring manager who had a role to fill. They had a woman candidate who was superbly qualified for the role and was within the budget that was set out for the salary. But there was also a man who was overqualified for the role and cost much more. They ended up hiring the man because they said, "Oh, he's got extra useful skills." This is an organisation trying to move towards gender balance and yet you've still got hiring managers doing things like that!'

'That sounds like a similar story I heard from my wife,' Steve replied. 'A company had a choice between a woman within budget and a man asking for a significantly higher salary. Both had excellent qualifications and experience, but they went for the man. And after a few months, he left.'

'That does make me laugh. But seriously, there seems to be something that makes companies want to pay more for someone typical compared with going with someone different. Is it bias? I think probably, yes.'

Steve nodded.

Markus continued, 'You know, this reminds me of something I heard a few weeks ago from Sana. She works in our operations department.'

***

'Have you felt excluded by your team?'

'Sometimes,' Sana replied. 'There was this time recently when a manager in my line asked me how old I am.'

'He did?! Well, we know he shouldn't have asked you that. I'm sorry that happened to you.'

'It's fine, it actually happens quite regularly that managers ask me how old I am. Each time they are surprised that I am older than I look, and each time they tell me I need to tell people.'

'Why would they say that?'

'Oh, well, on one occasion he said I had been discounted from certain roles because they thought I didn't have enough experience due to my perceived age.'

Markus couldn't believe his ears.

***

'That's disappointing. Trying something new or taking a risk was one of those psychological safety questions, wasn't it?' Steve asked.

'Yes, that's one of them.'

'So bringing in someone different into a team would be trying something new. Maybe psychological safety comes into play also then? Do people feel judged on who they bring into a team?'

'That's one to think about. What I think organisations need to look at is: Are they "walking the talk"? If they say they want a gender-balanced organisation, are they checking to see if everyone is aligned on that? Are they making the time to do so or focusing on quick responses that usually mean more of the same?'

'Good questions, Markus. I'll admit, we often have to recruit quickly to meet customer needs, and yes, it is easier to make a decision on someone who we may know or has similar experiences to others in the team.' Steve sighed. He thought about how often he has pushed his team to close out their recruitment process to get new hires started… and how many opportunities to bring in a fresh perspective that he may have overlooked. 'Perhaps there is something my organisation can do in this space, I will look into it.'

'That's great, Steve. Any small change we can make will have positive impacts. Then when it comes to working in a team or organisation itself, women need to have the right environment around them, where they can grow and develop.'

'Yes, agreed. I would like to think we have that here, but we do have a problem motivating and retaining the women employees in our organisation, particularly those in STEM roles. This is one of the reasons I was keen to work with you on this, Markus.'

'Well, I have a few more examples that may help. Katrina, who has worked in the energy industry for five years post-graduation, shared her view with me.'

***

'I often feel it doesn't matter if I work or not,' said Katrina. 'My manager doesn't value the work I do and gives all the challenging scope to others in the team.'

'But is the work you are doing important?'

'Not at all. If I don't do the work I'm assigned, it wouldn't matter at all as it makes no difference.'

'That's not good. Have you spoken with your manager about this?'

'Yes, and he said he'd look at it, but nothing seems to change.'

***

Markus said, 'It was hard to hear this one as I know how stretched the industry is at the moment to find people with the right skills, and here is someone with a great skill set not being utilised or enabled to grow.'

'This sounds similar to what we discussed this morning about, what was it, "office housework", when all they give her to do is that. It is detrimental to the business – it seems that too many managers are unaware of the negative impact their behaviour has on the business.'

'And I don't think it's just the managers or team leads themselves that are the issue. It can be the culture itself that is pretty toxic. Tahmina in software development mentioned something similar to me. She noticed a bug in the software that was quite complicated to explain. When she flagged it with the lead developer, a man, he proceeded to argue with her – he was convinced she was wrong. She ended up making a video showing how the code operated, including the error, and sent it to him. Tahmina spent about two hours trying to convince him of the bug because he couldn't accept that she had found something that he had missed.'

'Again, I start wondering if this man felt threatened by her, or maybe she approached it the wrong way – in a "look what I found" way – that could have made him defensive.'

'Perhaps. I didn't get an indication if that was how she approached it, but I agree that wouldn't have been the most effective approach. How you approach something is just as important as what you have to say about it.'

'Yes, exactly, I've seen some women go about things completely the wrong way and they wonder why they don't get the outcome they want.'

'But remember we talked about how men and women can be perceived differently for doing the same thing. Did you ever see that shampoo commercial on stereotypes? If not, I'll send you the link. They compare men and women doing the same thing and the different perceptions – boss for a man and bossy for a woman. You should take a look.'

'Yes, send it to me and I will.'

Pantene 'Labels Against Women' Digital Ad (2013): https://www.youtube.com/watch?v=luLkfXixBpM

'Anyway,' Markus continued, 'there is an element of self-awareness that I think everyone could benefit from. One of the questions I asked a woman called Narmin about was how women see themselves and how it differs from men. She's an electrical engineer and shared her thoughts on this at one of the ERG events. She said, "It's about the spectrum of female attributes to male attributes. Maybe it's a biological thing – women have children and are therefore protective, very aware of their environment and the dangers around them." Whereas she says, "men tend to bluster into a room, say what they want and leave."'

'I suppose I've seen that,' Steve replied.

'She went on to say that historically men were the hunter gatherer using their adrenaline response, but that no longer translates into the office environment today. Women tend to see the interactions around them, they are more attuned. Women say things like: "Did you see the way that person lifted their eyebrow?" She said she's never heard a man say things like that.'

'What did she mean, "lifted their eyebrow"?'

'I think she meant reading the room, seeing the micro-expressions from those in the meeting.'

'But why does that matter?' Steve probed. 'In a business meeting, the things that need to be said get said and we move on. What else is there?'

'I think it's the same point that women can behave differently and are therefore perceived differently. But the different abilities, such as reading the room, may make building relationships slightly easier, for example. If they can see someone is making expressions that imply that they are not happy about something but don't say it, it could be something worth discussing to improve the relationship further down the line.'

'That could be something beneficial. If there is a team member who has a special "superpower" that can help, then we absolutely must ensure they are enabled to do so.'

'But there are good examples, too. I have seen when a senior leader advocated for a woman joining the team and introduced her explaining her skill set, experience, and why she was such a great addition to the team. It made a real difference in how the team treated her due to the senior leader using his political capital.'

'That sounds straightforward enough, but doesn't that happen anyway? I've always seen that with new team members.'

'Were the new team members women?'

'Well... now that I think about it, I can't think of a time when it was a woman,' Steve replied quietly.

Markus continued, 'Leading with curiosity is another good technique based on another woman I spoke with called Jess.'

***

'I started a new project manager role where I joined a very technical team working on a programme of solutions for a laboratory,' said Jess. 'My role was to implement new project management processes. The programme was run by a man and we worked together really effectively.'

'Really? What was it that made your relationship so effective?'

'At the start we sat down to explore how to navigate the processes with the team and very quickly he started to understand what a project manager does. The team was brilliant, really technically excellent, and great to work with. I remained friends with many of them long after the scope was complete.'

'What was it the team did that made the difference?'

'I think it was mainly due to the team being open, curious, respectful, and humble. Embracing someone with a fresh perspective in an area new to them was crucial. They didn't question my competence, they accepted that I came in to add value in a different area, and once we worked out who did what, it worked perfectly.'

***

'This is a great example of how embracing someone different can be successful by working under the assumption that the person is competent,' Markus added.

'Yes, exactly, and we need to encourage more of that. It's strange that something as simple as this isn't normal practice.'

'Agreed, but we can do something about that.'

'Yes, we can. Time for a short break before we wrap up for the day?'

∗∗∗

Organisational leaders have a number of issues to resolve to ensure their employees are included. In many cases, bias drives exclusion from teams, which can impact someone's view on the new person's technical skills and value they can bring to the team. Unfortunately, as referenced in the stereotypes video (Pantene, 2013), a man and woman can be doing the same thing but are perceived very differently by others. Women in STEM have frequently reported experiences of this kind of bias. Over time, someone who is excluded and not valued for the work they do will become demotivated and disengaged. This can be resolved, though, and it takes good leadership to turn it around. Advocating for newcomers to the team and acknowledging the value they bring to the team is critical.

Top Tips for Organisations:

- ✤ Check for bias when hiring, particularly when selecting a candidate, and don't rush. If someone different from the norm meets the requirements, be confident in taking a chance on them.
- ✤ Check with your employees that the work they are doing is meaningful and impactful, and how it motivates them.

- Promote an environment where if one team member does well it reflects well on the whole team in order to remove negative behaviours driven by ego. Recognising others' skill sets that complement others in the team is critical.
- Encourage senior leaders to practise advocacy for those who are different in the team to ensure their capabilities are recognised.

Top Tips for Women:

- When highlighting a concern, ensure focus stays on impact to the business and the solution required. Avoid blaming individuals.
- Be mindful that many men will not pick up on subtleties in meetings, where things go unsaid. When bringing it up, keep it objective and focus on the impact.
- Stay curious, ask lots of questions to understand other perspectives, and encourage others to do the same.

Summary of part 2

Recognising existing talent within the organisation is key to any business's continued success. As it reaches the end of the day, Markus and Steve return from their break and start reflecting on their discussions. It has now been six months since they initially met, and their reciprocal mentoring agreement is seen by both as an effective use of time.

***

'It's been another good day! We have covered a lot about how women in STEM are, or rather could be, better valued for their technical skills and performance.'

'Yes,' Steve replied, 'it has been quite interesting to hear these real examples of how women continue to be excluded, and often it is from the very purpose of bringing them in – to bring a different perspective!'

'It would be great if women didn't frequently have imposter syndrome. I'm sure there will be men who question their own capabilities, but it appears to be much more prevalent among women. In the case of women in STEM, doubting their own abilities is one thing, but to be actively excluded or only recognised for low-level activities when they are capable of so much more is destructive over time.'

'And they will end up leaving the organisation.'

'Yes, and then we're back to square one.'

'We need teams that recognise this issue. We need teams that are mindful of office housework and consciously distribute the work across the team – that's how they'll improve their business performance.'

'And teams that will recognise and praise others when work gets done – even ostensibly simple work may take much longer to complete than they realise.'

'But as you pointed out,' Steve added, 'it needs to be real, authentic feedback. Not praise for the sake of it as that undermines the intent. Recognition is exactly that – recognising the effort someone puts in. It may take a more experienced person a fraction of the time to complete it, but for someone learning, it may be a big success for them that they managed it.'

'That's absolutely true. We also need to encourage regular, constructive feedback for all, really. And promote an environment where people feel comfortable giving and receiving feedback, knowing its purpose is to move the person forward.'

'And people need to be mindful of bias,' Steve said, as he checked his notes. 'Bias could come from the feedback provider or indeed the receiver.'

'Yes, that's right, too, and to combat that, the organisation could look into unconscious bias training. Speaking of that, did you find out any more about the course your organisation ran?'

'Oh, yes, we didn't cover that, did we? I spoke with our HR girl about the course. She said as the course was optional, there wasn't a big take-up, and the ones who did sign up were ones who were already involved in diversity and inclusion initiatives.'

'Steve – "girl" again?'

'Sorry, Markus, I'm trying. You know, old habits die hard.'

'But you know it's better not to refer to women as "girls"– you wouldn't want someone to refer to you as a boy! Anyway, that feedback doesn't sound great. Did your HR rep have any suggestions for what to do next?'

'She suggested including it in some future leadership training programme that is required for all. She thinks it will catch those who need it, and it would also be a continuous element throughout the programme, where leaders can reflect their learnings on a regular basis. Experiential learning, she called it.'

'That sounds like a good idea. I would be interested in knowing how that goes.'

'I think it's still some way out, but I will keep you updated as I hear more.'

'As well as bias, my next takeaway was to showcase role models. Perhaps those with different backgrounds – did we talk about that? My thinking is showing how perhaps senior leaders are actually all quite different in ways probably no one has thought to ask. That could be a good exercise in showcasing difference.'

'I don't think we covered that, but that's OK, we did talk about making sure women have meaningful work, which I suppose follows on from the office housework, but in this case it was more about ensuring they aren't "pigeonholed" into something that they can go beyond.'

'Yes, and making sure their skills that are unique to the team are acknowledged and utilised to make the team even better.'

'And have leaders advocate for those who may be overlooked.'

'This has been a great session today,' said Markus cheerfully. 'I have a lot to think about and lots of ideas of how to include this in the work we're doing in my organisation.'

'Yes, same here, I will be passing these on to my leadership team and HR, and I want to know they take these into account when building future training offerings.'

'Well, it was great to see you, Steve. I look forward to our next session.'

***

Markus and Steve have been very active during this check-in. When they met last quarter, Steve was attentive during the discussions. However, today he offered opinions and advice, which shows that he is much more engaged with this topic. Steve can see a clear connection between inclusion of the right skills and business performance.

However, while Markus is regularly meeting with his colleagues and women in STEM external to his organisation, Steve, by contrast, plans to delegate his ideas to his team. It is uncertain at this time how likely Steve is to follow up with his team on their progress as he hasn't taken direct ownership of any commitments.

Inclusion of the right skills can be easier to approach with more traditional managers, who focus primarily on the needs of the business. However, where managers are more focused on their self-image, they may not take the appropriate time to get to know their team members, including their individual needs and aspirations. This is where organisations need to set clear expectations of their leaders and how they interact with their teams, including recognition of work, providing feedback, and advocacy.

PART 3

EMPOWER YOUR FUTURE LEADERS

During the summer months, Markus takes some time off to spend with his family. He tells Isabella about all the women he has met with since the start of the year and describes how important their skills are to the world. Markus sees Isabella light up as he describes these role models – if they can do it, she can, too.

Steve has had a busy summer. There are upcoming organisational changes planned at his company and many of his colleagues are concerned how this will impact them. Steve has been working with his leadership team to discover ways they can motivate their teams and has also spent a lot of time with his customers to reaffirm his organisation's commitment to them. The focus on the women-retention initiatives has been deprioritised by Steve, but he remains committed to the reciprocal mentoring sessions with Markus.

Steve visits Markus's offices in September.

***

'Steve – did you get that email last week about the Women in STEM awards in December? We are sponsoring one of the categories this year and will have a table. Are you going?'

'Oh, yes, I saw that email. It's been a busy time lately, so I haven't thought much about it, but, yes, I plan to attend. It was a good night last year, wasn't it?'

'Yes, it was. That's good you'll be attending. Anyway, I was thinking about this session a fair bit over the last few weeks. Leadership is a big topic, and I thought of a few different ways we could carve this one out. What were you thinking?'

'Well, it's very important to have the right leadership in any organisation. And when you want to make any change, but especially in the culture of the workplace, it is critical that the right leaders are in place.'

'Yes, agreed. I was thinking about traditional leadership of the past. You know, the command-and-control types, in their ivory towers, alpha males. As time has progressed, we're seeing leaders becoming more available to their teams, moving away from command-and-control to a more democratic leadership style.'

'Well, in some industries, yes, but I'm sure command-and-control is still the style of choice for certain industries, and particularly in certain countries and cultures,' Steve replied.

'That's true. For some, an autocratic leadership style is effective and accepted. But for others it can be problematic. One woman told me about a company where she used to work where the founder would openly say sexist and inappropriate things, but he felt he was untouchable as he was the CEO.'

'Well, from what I've seen over time, things always catch up to you, one way or the other. And these days with social media, all it would take is for someone with a phone to record the CEO being inappropriate and it can be the end of a company.'

'That's a very real risk today for those leaders,' Markus replied. 'Anyway, where businesses have opted for a different style of leadership, it can provide opportunities for their employees that they wouldn't have had before. For example, junior employees can now spend time with their leaders to learn more about their career path and their values.'

'Are junior employees interested in that?'

'The ones I speak to are. They want to know how similar or different their leaders are to themselves – and what changes, if any, they need to make to reach the same position as their leaders or an equivalent. Leaders are role models.'

Steve thought for a moment. 'I always thought about leaders guiding their junior employees. You know, coaching them, mentoring them. Do I think of myself, for example, as a role model? You know, it hadn't crossed my mind before.'

'Your team will be watching you. Seeing what you deem acceptable or unacceptable, where you intervene, what you let slide, what you encourage. It sets the tone. Lots of people today, women included, want to work for leaders who inspire them. Leaders who share their values. Leaders who help them progress their careers.'

'It seems that it isn't just leadership that has changed in the past few decades. It seems the whole concept of work has changed and continues to change. Work used to be about making money, but today it can be more about status and purpose, and then of course, money.'

'Or sometimes when people understand their own purpose, they choose a job and company that aligns with it,' Markus replied. 'And if you're in a company where your purpose aligns with that of the business, you want to ensure you have all possible opportunities to add value and make positive impacts on the world.'

'Yes, that would be the ideal scenario. And you will need leaders that enable that type of environment.'

'And building up the next generation of leaders. Making sure they know leadership is not just a title, that if a leader has no followers, they aren't really a leader, and knowing how to identify the next lot of leaders.'

'Agreed, you want leaders who act ethically, create an environment where everyone feels included and connected to the business, and a leader who advocates for their team members to become future leaders.'

'Yes, exactly that. How about that as our framework for today?'

'Sounds good,' Steve replied. 'Now, remind me, which way to the coffee station?'

Chapter 7

Ethical leaders do the right thing

Organisations look to their leaders to set the tone by making it clear what is acceptable, what is not, and following it themselves. But how often do we see this in practice in the workplace? Historically, in many corporate organisations, if doing the right thing meant a negative outcome for the business, the person who raised the issue and took action would be reprimanded. However, today, many organisations encourage their employees to speak up when something is not right.

While there are many different leadership styles, one element that team members notice is when their leader takes an unethical approach. This is likely to create distrust in the team, and depending on the severity, may compromise any psychological safety that exists. While it may be difficult, and have short-term negative consequences, a leader that does the right thing ethically will ultimately gather more respect.

***

'When I think about great leaders I've worked for or around,' Markus said, 'I think of how they were as people. Even today when I think of whom I want to work for, I want it to be someone who is fair and supportive, but also challenging and honest.'

'And you want them to be clear on business needs,' Steve added.

'Yes, it makes a big difference when you work for someone who understands that and can give you clarity on how your part contributes, and what outcome is needed. And you want the team to be working as one in support of those business needs.'

'Yes, that is essential for any business.'

'But what we've mentioned in our previous discussions was this concept of competition within the team. Remember when we spoke about James and how he felt threatened by anyone taking the spotlight away from him?'

'Yes, I remember that. Definitely not the style of leadership we're after, or actually anyone in the team behaving like that.'

'Yes, exactly, and that is something you would need a leader to recognise, acknowledge, and resolve before the environment becomes toxic.'

'Although as I'm thinking, Markus, I have seen many times where healthy competition can help team members perform beyond their limits and provide even better results.'

'That's true, and if it is in support of the business goals then, yes, competition can be healthy. What I have heard from a lot of women though is the concept of "tall poppy syndrome".'

'What is that?'

'It is when someone is doing really well and they're seen as standing out from their peers,' Markus replied. 'They become figuratively taller than the rest. Others become resentful of the attention and "cut them down to size", figuratively speaking.'

'I thought it was just the press that did that to people?! But seriously, what makes people react like that? Is it jealousy?'

'It could be. It could be that they feel overlooked and can see someone else getting the limelight. Or maybe they don't feel that person deserves the attention – there could be many reasons.'

'That wouldn't be a nice team to be part of. You'd always be on the lookout. You want to do well, but not too well, otherwise you'll alienate yourself from the team.'

'Yes, exactly,' Markus replied. 'We need leaders who will recognise this when it happens and take action as that is the ethical thing to do even if it means short-term disruption in the team.'

'What could they do, though, to avoid the issue in the first place?'

'Well, one option could be to ensure all successes are celebrated by the group. I used to work with an agility coach who would encourage successes to be celebrated during a group meeting and would encourage a round of applause from all.'

'That sounds easy enough,' Steve replied. 'Recognition is something we are always trying to promote, but often gets overlooked.'

'Yes, and if we can make a point to applaud the team whenever any individual team member has a success, they will be more encouraged to support each other. Another option is to ensure when the individual is successful that they make sure they recognise those who helped them – it is rare that anyone succeeds only by themselves.'

'That's another good idea, Markus. I do wonder though, is this, "tall poppy syndrome", specific to women?'

'I don't think it is, but women in male-dominated environments are more likely to stand out anyway, which then means any recognition of success may be amplified in the eyes of someone who wants to put them down. And it isn't just men who do it to women.'

'What? Women do this to other women?' Steve asked, visibly indignant. 'Oh, was this what you called the queen bees?'

'Yes, it's them again. I spoke with a woman called Sophia about this very topic. She works in data science in a male-dominated organisation, but there are a small number of senior women.'

***

'I was invited to a meeting with two vice presidents, two of three women on the leadership team. I thought it was great that I had an opportunity to speak with them on a topic I am really passionate about – gender equity initiatives.'

'That sounds interesting,' Markus replied. 'How did the meeting go?'

'There were three meetings in total – each worse than the one before.'

'Why, what happened?'

'Well, previously a team of about eight women had created a plan for the gender equity initiatives for the following year. It had been endorsed by the VP and senior VP at the time, and presented at the final community meeting for the year. But the following year, there was a change in leadership and the decision was not to implement the plan.'

'Was there an explanation as to why?'

'Not really, just that they wanted to avoid having any pressure on the team to implement the plan.'

'So what happened next at your current meetings?'

'I had a different view of what the two VPs had proposed and one of them in particular did not value my questions. Essentially, she suggested group sharing sessions to build a community.'

'Is that not a good idea?'

'It's not that I thought it wasn't a good idea, but I questioned what the outcome was that we wanted by doing that. She wasn't able to answer me other than saying sharing stories and experiences. I have experience of that. It can become unstructured and become a place to go to complain about experiences rather than looking at it proactively to identify trends and propose solutions for improvement. I then decided to show her the examples of activities the team had come up with previously, but she wasn't interested.'

'Why do you think she wasn't interested?'

'I'm not sure. It would have been something we could measure, but when I suggested measuring progress, her response to me was: "Not everyone is as ambitious and career-driven as you are, Sophia!" I was taken aback especially as that was only the second hour I had ever spent with her.'

'Maybe she was having a bad day? It doesn't sound like she was listening to your suggestions.'

'It definitely felt like she was putting me in my place. I didn't know ambition was a bad thing, but I also don't think she knew me well enough to understand my ambitions or intentions. I spoke with one of my mentors, a man, about the situation. He said she may have felt threatened by me. It wasn't something I had thought of, but now thinking about it, she was new in role, of course wanted to make a good impression, and wanted to do something that she knew couldn't fail. And here I was picking holes in it and therefore needed to be swatted.'

'So what happened after that?'

'I wasn't invited to the future meetings and I haven't been involved since. It is very disappointing because this is a passion of mine. I've ended up looking further afield to see how I can add value in this area if my immediate team is not interested in me being involved.'

***

'It's strange, isn't it? You would think that women would support women especially in male-dominated fields. You know, those in the same tribe protecting each other?'

Markus smiled. 'Is that the same as saying all guys support each other?' Markus asked.

'Well, yes, I see what you mean, but you would hope that anyone in the same boat or having similar experiences or challenges would help others with the same.'

'From what I've heard, sometimes women who have achieved senior positions in traditionally male-dominated organisations like being the "only one". And when another woman comes along whom they see as a threat, they take action.'

'That doesn't sound very ethical.'

'No, it isn't. And ultimately the bullying results in people leaving the team. But I do have an example of a good experience. Mia is a project engineer who told me she's been quite lucky. She once had a new manager, a woman, who after a few weeks told her, "I want you to be better than me and do it faster than me." Mia said it immediately removed any suggestion of competition between them and created a sense of openness that they could discuss issues and challenges without feeling that one of them succeeding meant the other did not.'

'I think that should go without saying, but evidently it needs saying.'

'Yes, it appears that there is now a culture where everyone is looking for their own validation. We spoke about male allies before, but sometimes you just need allies, in general. Women can absolutely support other women without thinking it works against them if they are not the one in the spotlight.'

'And I'm sure there will be men in the same category.'

'Well, yes, I have heard of men sidelining women who are getting too much exposure. But I also had a man tell me, "My manager has all but explicitly told me he doesn't want me on the team and thinks I'm too young to have the visibility I have."'

'Age creeping up again?' Steve asked. 'I don't understand this – if someone is good enough, they are old enough. Age shouldn't come into it as long as they can do the job.'

'Unfortunately, it still seems to be more common than either of us would like. I get the feeling that some people don't want anyone to have an advantage that they didn't have. Or even just a perceived advantage. But it can get quite toxic. Sammie, who works as a development engineer in another organisation, told me about one of her experiences.'

***

'I didn't have the best experience with my manager. He liked to ask multiple people to do the same thing and see who finished first. Once I realised, I would check with others in my team whenever he asked me to do something. When someone else was already on it, I would leave them to it and not waste my time.'

'Why do you think he did that?'

'I think he lived in a world where competition was everywhere. But he also liked to put people down. On one occasion I found out that a contractor in my team had forged my signature on his time sheet. I informed my manager who said, "Well, no one has ever done that to me so you need to think about what you are doing and why he thought that was OK."'

'He said what?' Markus asked, visibly surprised.

'Yes, his response wasn't great. Eventually the whole thing was dealt with by my manager, his manager, and the company the contractor worked for. It wasn't raised to HR. When a decision was reached, my manager called me in and told me they were going to keep the contractor because his action was out of character. Not too long afterwards, the same guy was made staff and is now my peer.'

***

'There are a few things that concern me there. If someone speaks up to their manager about an issue that concerns a code of conduct issue like that, the manager should not turn it back on the person raising the issue,' Steve said. 'That is a sure sign of a toxic manager. Did she mention if her manager was a man or woman... Although I don't suppose it matters in this case?'

'She said her manager was a man.'

'Well, in any case I don't think he behaved ethically as it wouldn't encourage her to raise future issues – and that could result in significant reputational issues to the business.'

'Yes, exactly.'

'The next concern I have is why it wasn't raised to HR. Another violation. The issue with that is there wasn't any investigation and it becomes a "he-said-she-said" situation. And, yes, it doesn't surprise me that no action was taken, because no investigation means nothing formally documented.'

'Ethical issues all over this. But also, it probably didn't make Sammie feel very supported.'

'Well, exactly. I can imagine many people, men or women, if they were in a situation like that, it wouldn't take them long before they left the team.'

'So that is another reason for demotivation and ultimately attrition, especially of women. I found the sheer number of stories from these women quite concerning. Have you heard many stories like this from your discussions?'

Steve shifted uncomfortably.

'It's been busy lately, Markus, and I haven't had as much time as I would have liked to speak with the women in my organisation. We are still committed to moving the dial, though, and these sessions really help me to identify areas we can target.'

'Oh, that's OK, Steve, it's a marathon, not a sprint. Thinking about the underlying causes we've discussed, I wonder how those team members would assess the level of respect within their team.'

'Where are you going with that one?'

'If all team members respected each other, then if an issue was raised, they wouldn't ignore it, at least I would hope they wouldn't. But if they didn't respect the person raising it, or didn't respect their point of view, then I could see them pushing the issue, and the person, aside.'

'I see what you mean,' Steve replied. 'So what you're saying is, respect leads to ethical action. So are we promoting respectful cultures within our organisations?'

'Yes, I think something like that definitely needs to be considered,' Markus replied. 'Respect within the team, respect for the leadership, the leadership respecting the team.'

'And that last story didn't show the leader respecting the woman who raised the time sheet issue to him. A more respectful response would have been to thank her for raising the issue and then take it to HR – that would have been the most straightforward response that keeps everyone right.'

'There are a lot of people that don't like going to HR,' Markus replied. 'I've heard it both within and outside my organisation.'

'Why is that?'

'There's a feeling that it counts as a negative if you go to HR. Of course, no organisation supports this theory and acting in accordance with the organisation's code of conduct is promoted. But there is still this view, and it prevents people from doing the right thing.'

'Another roadblock for acting ethically. Thinking back to one of our previous sessions, you mentioned role models, Markus. That's what we need here – leaders who can share when they've gone to HR and how it hasn't negatively impacted their careers or reputations.'

'That's a great idea, Steve. Definitely one to capture.'

'And as well as that, we need leaders who aren't threatened by the success of their team members. They need to understand that organisations thrive on the success of their people. Without the best ideas, whoever they come from, the business won't succeed.'

'What we need is for people, men or women, to feel part of a team,' Markus suggested. 'As you say, a teammate's success is your success. Some organisations try this at company level through bonuses, but it doesn't give them that emotional connection. It needs to be from those with whom they work closely, where they support each other when there are challenges and celebrate together when there are successes.'

'Yes, exactly. And it's even better when someone has an idea or solution that no one else has come up with. It's better for the business and that's the most important thing.'

'And you don't want leaders who shut down those new ideas. Sammie said her manager used to argue with anyone who had a different idea from his own.'

Steve shook his head.

Markus continued, 'Then if the person persisted, he would say negative things about the person challenging him to anyone who would listen – even if they didn't know the person.'

'You wonder how people like that get into positions of leadership.'

'Maybe he just said the right thing to the right people?'

'Organisations need to do better to make sure they have the right kind of leaders. Those who do the right thing ethically.'

'Yes, and we need leaders, and teams, who challenge themselves to think outside the box, too. I knew a leader who said he deliberately chose team members who filled the gaps he had in his skills.'

'Really?' Steve asked. 'How did he know if they were doing a good job then if he didn't understand what they did?'

'He had a different style. He focused on knowing the people, building trust such that when there was a problem, they would tell him. He could then escalate issues, bring in experts, and so on, to help the team.'

'It's certainly a different approach than I've seen.'

'I would call it authentic humility,' Markus replied. 'Where someone is being upfront and honest about what they know and don't know, and they're in an environment where they won't be judged negatively for it.'

'A psychologically safe environment.'

'Yes, exactly, and it's not just leaders. You want all team members to celebrate new skill sets and diverse thinking. That sounds like a team I want to be in. Now, shall we head down to the canteen and grab some lunch?'

***

Leaders have a critical role to play in organisations when it comes to their people. Their behaviours can be mirrored by their employees, therefore they need to be mindful of this even when they have a bad day. It is important for their leaders to behave ethically in the same way as they expect others to behave. It can be difficult for traditional leaders to assess their leadership style and adapt to a more modern approach, but today's workforce demands it.

Markus and Steve have identified several good suggestions based on what they have seen working with great leaders in the past or through their own learning over their careers. A common theme among the best leaders is the positivity that their employees feel, and particularly when they take the right ethical or moral action – it gains respect. The top tips below can be used to help establish positive and respectful relationships through recognition and visibility.

Top Tips for Organisations:

- Promote a respectful environment where successes of any team members are recognised and supported as reflections on the team – this should help to mitigate any signs of 'tall poppy syndrome' or 'queen bees'.
- Consider showcasing role models who have 'spoken up' or reported code of conduct breaches to HR without any negative impacts to their careers or reputation.

⚝ Recognise leaders who lead by example by practising and promoting authentic humility.

Top Tips for Women:

⚝ Recognise those who have been integral to your success.

⚝ Feel confident when raising an issue, knowing you have taken an ethical approach.

⚝ If you are in a leadership position, seek to lift others as you rise. This could include men as well as other women.

Chapter 8

Diversity means nothing without inclusion

Women have frequently reported occurrences of being told they only got the job because of their gender, or to meet DEI targets. Sometimes it is said directly to them and at other times it is discussed behind their back. While senior leaders condemn attitudes like this and encourage anyone impacted to speak up, it is rare that serious action is taken.

Often the focus on meeting diversity targets takes precedence over any focus on improving workplace culture to be more inclusive. For example, individuals are often promoted into leadership roles without any formal leadership assessment. The decision to move them into a role leading people is often development driven and can be due to good performance as an individual contributor. However, the skill sets to be an effective leader are very different to engineering delivery roles, for example. This can result in a leader that is unaware of and may be missing several key leadership skills, including an understanding of how to create an inclusive culture within a team. Equally, if the organisation does not evaluate a leader's ability to create an inclusive culture in the team, there may be no motivation for that leader to focus on this area.

***

Over lunch, Markus and Steve spoke about changes taking place in their respective organisations. Steve's organisation is going through a reorganisation that is likely to take until the end of the year. Markus's has been through several reorganisations, but other than changing titles and reporting lines, he's never noticed real difference in the organisational culture.

'Markus, you speak a lot about the environment and culture of organisations. How do you think organisations can get to that place?' Steve asked on their way back from lunch.

'Well, I think it would take a fair bit of time, depending on the existing culture of the organisation. Personally, I think a lot of the culture comes from the top. I regularly see CEOs and other very senior leaders of organisations making speeches about what their organisation is doing to change the industry or the world. What I always wonder is how much that message resonates with others throughout the organisation.'

'I take it you mean more than just communicating the message?'

'Yes, I'm thinking about what the organisation sees their leaders do. Take, for instance, the gender quotas we hear a fair bit about. A lot of companies talk about their gender pay gap, what they are doing to improve gender equity, all the good optics, but how much real progress have they made since they first started talking about it? Are women being paid more but still being sidelined and doing the "office housework"? What is really changing?'

'I'm sure each company is trying their best, Markus.'

'I understand that, but equally, if the senior leaders say one thing and do something else, it won't be long until people notice. Diversity is so much more than just a tick box. Katya, who works in a product design company, shared her view on this with me.'

***

'How do you feel about how your leaders drive the organisation's diversity, equity, and inclusion efforts?'

'I think they try,' Katya replied, 'but it doesn't feel very real or authentic.'

'In what way?'

'You know when you get the feeling someone is doing something only because they have been told to or because it is expected of them? It's a bit like that. My organisation is driving an initiative to bring in more women and more people from under-recognised groups as a priority. It is spoken about all the time, progress on meeting the quotas is constantly monitored, and all people development discussions are steered by it. A lot of my colleagues feel very alienated and have raised it at town halls, but the company keeps going regardless.'

'Have you seen any changes due to the drive for diverse hires?'

'Nothing positive. I've seen some women join the organisation and then after some time, many of those who had been brought in leave – they either resigned or were fired.'

'Really?' Markus asked, visibly surprised. 'What caused that to happen?'

'I only knew a few of the women directly, but it was always the same story. They weren't included or listened to, and those who raised that as an issue were fired or moved aside until they left of their own accord.'

***

'Was that company looking for a lawsuit?' Steve asked rhetorically. 'You would think companies today would know better. Quotas are not the answer, which is why many companies have moved to using the word "targets" instead. I suppose "target" sounds more aspirational.'

'Yes, "quotas" sounds much more mandated. But in any case, adding women or any other under-recognised groups as tick boxes is counter-intuitive in my view. Diversity is one thing, but without inclusion – actively including new ways of thinking – there seems little point.'

'Not to mention the cost it takes to hire and train personnel.' Steve thought some more then asked, 'But how can leaders do better? I understand they can set the target – the goal for increasing representation – but then they would expect their team to make plans to meet it, which roll down to their team's respective teams, etc. Is that not how you would do it?'

'It's one approach. In an ideal world, I see women's ideas being just as valued as men's ideas within the team. Rather than women being there to "tick a diversity box", they have their personal purpose and the business purpose aligned, and care about their team's objectives, which means their ideas and suggestions will come from a place of driving business improvements.'

'But you don't want to disrupt the status quo of the team. And you don't want those who have been in the organisation for some time to feel alienated and to pander to these newfangled ideas – that would make any man want to leave, which would increase recruitment costs again!'

'It requires tact from the leader, Steve, and setting the tone as we talked about earlier. And for that, you'd need a leader who understands this. I wonder sometimes if organisations assess people before they put them into leadership positions.'

'What do you mean, Markus?'

'Well, other than the senior managers, I don't often hear mid-level leaders talking about diversity, equity, and inclusion as commonplace topics. But you really want leaders who understand why it is so important, especially for their team to develop and grow.'

Steve thought carefully. 'I know in my organisation it is expected that there is a lot of "on the job" training, but no, I don't believe there is an assessment of any kind before someone is put into a leadership role. It tends to be along the lines of giving someone a stretch opportunity to lead others and see how they get on.'

Markus smiled. 'And how does that work out?'

'You win some, you lose some. But what I'm taking from this conversation is that we need to ensure leaders are equipped with all the right tools to be effective with their team, and that includes a good understanding and appreciation of why inclusion is critical.'

'Yes, absolutely. Because if you think about it, one of the key purposes of a leader, as well as setting the vision and supporting the team, is to create future leaders, and for that, you need to include team members. From what I have learned from my research, it doesn't seem like all leaders have that understanding and mentality.'

'Building up future leaders takes time though,' Steve replied. 'And again, there's the balance between developing people and delivering on the business needs. Sometimes the business needs are so critical that everything else needs to take a back seat.'

'I understand, it's about balance, though, over a period of time. But thinking about people development with the lens of gender diversity, one idea suggested to me during my interviews was for companies to create a gender affinity network.'

'Is that the same as an employee resource group?'

'It is similar, the difference is in the name. I don't think anyone likes being referred to as a "resource". Using the term "affinity" shows it is a group of people with a natural liking or understanding of something, which more accurately describes what they are trying to do… in my opinion anyway.'

'That does seem to be a fair distinction between the two names. How successful are those kinds of networks?'

'Based on the women I have spoken with, what makes or breaks it is support from their leadership. Anytime a woman spoke positively about their experience in a gender affinity network, it was because they had leaders actively showing up and/or men being part of the network.'

'Men are part of the gender affinity network?! I've generally only seen women in networks like that.'

'Yes, men do take part, and it makes a big difference,' Markus replied. 'Men can bring diverse thinking into that network, too, and personally I have learned so much from joining in the network in my organisation. I found I could relate to a lot of the issues even though as a man I haven't experienced them myself.'

'It sounds like it has been positive for you, Markus, and for your organisation. But as a leader, how would you encourage other men to join in without sounding like you're mandating it or "ticking a box"?'

'That's where "walking the talk" comes in. If a leader sets a target around their gender ambition, and then is seen to actively take part in initiatives to meet that gender ambition, in my mind that makes them a role model. And you would know very quickly if they were being authentic or not.'

Steve thought on this for a moment. Could he see himself making the time to spend on gender ambition initiatives? Would he be thought of positively if he was seen to be spending time on that rather than focusing on the business and profits?

'I suppose the main thing is to ensure you have adequate leadership representation at those events, but we have a lot of men who have been in the industry for 20–30 years who don't want to change and don't understand why they need to change. This is often the sticking point where they walk away.'

'Yes, I have seen that happen. Someone I spoke with from another organisation told me their company ran two programmes for gender balance, a woman's programme to get more women leaders and train them, and a men's programme to ensure the men would understand why they need a programme for women, how they can support it, and play their part in managing the gender balance environment. They wanted the men to "walk the talk" as male allies.'

'You mentioned male allies previously, Markus. It isn't a term I am very familiar with. How would you describe a male ally?'

'I asked the same question just a few weeks ago! Tom, the consultant, describes three categories: 1. Leaning in, 2. Ally, and 3. Agent of change. Taking examples from our discussion: Awareness of unconscious bias would be categorised as leaning in, completing training on inclusive behaviours would be an example of being an ally, and behaving inclusively and promoting a psychologically safe environment would be an agent of change.'

Steve paused and thought about what he had heard. 'Do you have more of these examples?'

'Yes, I have a matrix. I'll send it to you after this.'

Men Leaning In Matrix

https://docs.google.com/presentation/d/1OovRRKb3
LbXDdLYZsMnixuugz74FtjJpU8-sBXc5nGg/edit#slide=
id.g184f34ba142_1_387

'Thanks. I haven't heard this before.'

'Neither had I. I spoke with a few of my male colleagues who felt a little deflated that they were only leaning in as they thought they were champions in inclusion.'

'I will have a look at the matrix when you send it through. Back to your earlier point though. You mentioned programmes that were run for men and for women – did they work?'

'They discovered a lot when running the programme for men,' Markus replied. 'Comments like "Women are taking our jobs", and they had to clarify – they weren't men's jobs in the first place, they are just jobs men happen to occupy.'

'I can imagine many organisations having men with similar comments.'

'Yes, I know I've heard it here. What the company also observed was the need to be very clear and objective about assessing who is selected for each role. Making data transparent was also very effective in showing the pace of promotion for women compared with the pace of promotion for men. Many men thought more women were being promoted than men until they saw the data. It is difficult to argue with the data.'

'And yet they still will!' Steve replied. 'You need to accept that some people won't change, and that's OK, not everyone needs to think the same way.'

Markus paused and thought carefully.

'I know you can't force someone to agree with you, but you do want people to want to create a positive environment for everyone. As we talked about in one of our previous sessions, I've heard women say they've been openly told by their peers they "only got the job because they're a woman", which of course wasn't the case. The implication is there was no consideration for her experience, skills, approach to situations, how she interacts with teams both internally and externally, and her career potential. Comments like that are damaging – they increase imposter syndrome and also there's no way someone said that without knowing how it would be taken.'

'Yes, of course, I didn't mean it like that,' Steve said hastily. 'What I meant was if companies focus on being competitive in the environment in which they operate, they will need to ensure effective and competitive skill sets for the future. Some will fit that box and others won't. In my experience, the ones who won't will eventually leave.'

'Yes, I guess if someone is fighting the changes and doesn't leave, that's when you get a problem. But I know if I were to imagine organisations in the future, I want to see a 50:50 gender split. I want to see leaders who are "people people", and who understand their employees. The culture at work is respectful, inclusive, and teams debate solutions until they reach the right one, regardless of who the idea comes from.'

'That sounds very achievable. What is holding that back?'

'Well, for starters, we need men with traditional views to acknowledge that organisations want leaders who under-stand gender balance, diversity, and inclusion. Organisations don't just want women leaders, they want a balance with 50% male, and those 50% will be those who support gender equity – not the ones who fight it. If those men want to be those leaders, they need to look at themselves and their skill sets to see which gaps they need to fill to be considered.'

'And that will be a challenge for some.'

Markus smiled. 'Yes, it's much easier to complain than to develop your skills,' Markus replied. 'But the organisation wants well-rounded employees – not just those with great technical skills.'

'Yes, agreed. Now, I need some caffeine. Let's grab a coffee and stretch our legs.'

***

Where leaders are not focused on women's ideas or concerns, it can result in disengagement, and particularly from those who already feel excluded from the team. Over time, disengaged women can bring negativity to the team, which can create even more disruption. Ultimately, those who are being overlooked or overworked will eventually leave the team and perhaps the organisation. Leaders who understand the need to focus on inclusion, and not just diversity, and who take action to engage everyone in the team, including the women, will be taking steps to improve their workplace culture and reduce attrition.

Steve is not in his comfort zone today. In his mind, he goes back to his more traditional frame of reference and is trying to see how Markus's suggestions can work within that framework. Often it can't as we saw when he considered being outspoken about gender ambition initiatives. In a lot of aspects, Steve needs to change his mindset from a command-and-control leader to one who empowers and supports the team where required. Markus in contrast has many ideas and is speaking from a place of empathy to those who have not had positive experiences with their leaders. He is getting involved within his organisation and striving to be an agent of change. Steve in contrast is struggling to meet any of the Men Leaning In Matrix examples. On the positive side, Steve has asked many questions to help him identify a path to take actions that Markus has suggested. Here are some top tips based on their discussion.

Top Tips for Organisations:

- ✠ Senior leaders should try to actively participate in the initiatives (e.g. gender affinity networks) that they promote, to underline the perception of junior employees that their leaders really think what they are promoting.
- ✠ Organisations should avoid mandating quotas for gender equity, which can negatively impact the perception of women when they receive a promotion. Instead, use of targets, transparency of data, and reasons why improvement in diversity is good for the business should be made clear and communicated regularly. One way for employees to find out more and to participate is through a gender affinity network.
- ✠ Focus on inclusion to improve business outcomes, and avoid bringing in new perspectives (i.e. more women) only to exclude them.
- ✠ Highlight the skills expected of future leaders in the organisation and encourage all to reflect on their gaps and how to close them.

⚜ Promote a culture where the best leaders create an environment in their team that is respectful, honest, open, and shows trust in more junior employees by providing autonomy.

Top Tips for Women:

⚜ Identify senior leaders that you respect and those from whom you would value their advice. Ask if they would consider mentoring you and nurture that relationship over time.

⚜ When reflecting on the type of leadership needed in the future, assess your own skills and identify any gaps that need to be closed.

⚜ Seek clarity on how your role contributes to the goals of the business. If it does not, find out what needs to be changed in order for you to make a positive impact.

⚜ Advise your manager if you wish for more autonomy to complete your work and ask what is needed to make that happen.

⚜ Encourage your male peers to take part in gender affinity networks, particularly if leaders are involved, as an opportunity to make new relationships.

Chapter 9

Trust and advocacy enable career progression

Trust is considered very important when reflecting on qualities valued in a great leader. Having a leader who is trusted and will support their team contributes significantly to the psychological safety within the team, which in turn improves productivity. How do we know when a leader is doing the right thing for their people? Those that are most likely to have a view will be their team and their direct reports. A leader can often make decisions that impact the team or individual team members but does not include the team in any discussions – for example, appointment of someone into a new position. In some cases, the decision may be received negatively. To retain respect to and from the team, a leader needs to ensure the team has enough knowledge to know decisions are made in the best interests of the organisation and therefore of the team. This relies on trust and trust relies on relationships.

Frequently, men build these relationships outside of the workplace and when it comes to support for a promotion or role change, advocacy from those individuals makes the difference. Women, though, can find it much more challenging to build these relationships with their leaders, which can hinder their career progression, resulting in stagnation and ultimately attrition.

***

During their coffee break, Markus and Steve spoke about their career trajectories and the leaders that had supported them. As they returned, they thought more about what makes great leadership and how it impacts an organisation.

'Markus, you mentioned earlier about leaders who know their junior employees. Are you thinking beyond those who just work directly for them?'

'Yes, definitely. Ideally you want leaders who are accessible, and those that have a good feel for the pulse of the organisation at different levels.'

Steve pondered on this point. It felt so foreign to think about getting close to those junior to him in the organisation. When he thought back over his career, all the organisational structures had been very hierarchical. He had even blazed his own trail by having lunch with those women in STEM in his organisation. Surely that was enough?

'How would you see a senior leader achieving that?'

'I mentor a few men and women at different levels in the organisation,' Markus replied. 'I know some very senior leaders that do the same. Sometimes it is reverse mentoring, sometimes just regular mentoring, but it builds relationships over time.'

'Oh, yes, I see. So selecting a few people to meet with and get to know them?'

'Sometimes it's the junior employee who makes contact for some advice or guidance. And then it's a case of seeing where it goes. Do they continue to set up meetings, or does it fall away? It depends on the chemistry between the participants and whether they feel they are benefiting from the interaction.'

'What do you feel you get out of those relationships?'

'I like to think I'm helping someone navigate their career in our organisation. Of course, they may not always follow my advice, but I remain available to them when challenges arise or if they want to test an idea with me. It also helps me when I discuss personnel decisions with my management or my team, as I then have a better idea of how it feels to walk in someone else's shoes.'

'What's the most common challenge they come to you with?' Steve probed.

'There are quite a few different things people have come to me about. But over time, I've noticed a few times that particularly women come to me to discuss their managers. More specifically, they want to find a way to have more autonomy in their work.'

'Autonomy? You mean they are being micromanaged?'

'Sometimes. Sometimes it is about feeling trusted to get on with their work and know that they'll ask for help if needed.'

'And their managers don't support that?'

'Often, I think they just overlook it,' Markus replied. 'If you bring in someone to your team, man or woman, then micromanage everything they do, it isn't surprising if the person ends up unhappy. I tend to find people want meaning in their work – knowing they are making a difference – and the autonomy to do so, as it shows they are trusted.'

'I can see how some managers, perhaps less experienced, may have difficulty handing the reins over to those who are more junior than they are. But if they have filled the team with people with the right skill sets, then they need to trust them to do their jobs.'

'Exactly. Yes, their reputation could be at risk, but as you said, if they have the right people in the team, and create the right environment where the team is honest and open about any challenges, the manager can intervene early, if needed, to help them. You know, when I think of great managers or leaders that I've worked for, I think of those people who I know had my back. I'm not sure if many women feel like that at work.'

'What makes you think that?' Steve asked.

'There were a few comments during my conversations. One woman wasn't convinced her manager ever spoke positively about her.'

'I doubt that would be the case. It would reflect badly on her manager if they were always negative about a junior employee. If managers have an issue with a junior employee, they should be able to identify solutions, and if not, seek the appropriate help from another manager or HR.'

'That's true,' Markus replied, 'but it can be difficult to just trust that your manager wants the best for you. Here we have a lot of discussions about personnel that only people at a certain level and in certain roles are permitted to attend. It's at those meetings that one of the things discussed is upcoming roles and who may be available to fill them.'

'Yes, I have heard feedback about lack of transparency in how we place people. We often tend to have a problem where we have roles but we don't have the right people to fill them, which means there's no time to explain to everyone what we're doing.'

'When you say right people, do you mean the right skill sets?'

'Yes, exactly. It's a recurring problem. I ask my leadership team when we have vacancies and most times there isn't time to train someone and we end up recruiting an external candidate.'

'It sounds like the development process in your organisation may need to be looked at. But I would also suggest checking how your employees are being assessed.'

'Do you think there could be a problem?'

'Well,' Markus replied, 'one of the points that came up during discussions was that often the women felt overlooked and not recognised for their skills, as we talked about last time. I wonder if there could be bias.'

'That's a good idea. I'll have a look into it. But back to your organisation. When you are looking to move internal candidates, aren't all roles advertised for people to apply?'

'Not always. Sometimes for specific development purposes, or if someone is in a particular location and has the right skill set, or for several other reasons, a certain person is identified for an upcoming vacancy. The people around the table have a discussion, ideally someone will speak with the individual to see if they are interested, and then there's a decision taken at the next meeting. The same group meets to discuss performance ratings – we have to align to a bell curve which means 60% of people get "average", 20% get "above average", and 10% get "top".

'What about the final 10%?' Steve asked.

'That's for those below average, but that one isn't mandated. Anyway, the group gets together and debates which team members get "above average" and "top" – that is where you need a manager who will speak for you as it directly impacts your performance rating, your pay, and your potential rating. I think a lot of companies use the bell curve for this purpose.'

'We do things differently in my organisation. Our performance ratings are done one-to-one between the junior-level employee and the manager and entail a discussion on what has gone well, what could have been better, and specific development areas. There's normally a list against which the manager assesses and then they total the score. That is how they define their performance rating.'

'So it's just between the junior employee and manager? That's different. I can see pros and cons of each approach. Both require the manager to know the junior employee or gather feedback on them to provide an unbiased view. I think having more than one person set the rating is a way of reducing any bias though.'

'But how does this impact women in STEM?' Steve asked.

'It's back to unconscious bias again. They can be at risk of receiving performance feedback that is biased, and it may delay their career progression. A lot seems to keep coming back to bias.'

'Well, what can a woman do to help herself?'

'Where possible, people need to control the narrative about them as much as they can. So what does that mean? Well, we have a development engineer call Gracie. I talked to her about it. She believed there were three steps a woman could take to control the narrative around her. The first was to identify the decision makers who will be in the room. The second was to build relationships with those decision makers and make it clear what those decision makers want and need, and third was to nurture and maintain those relationships.'

'Don't women do that already?'

'Not very often from what I've heard,' Markus replied. 'People in general, but especially women in STEM, need to appreciate that they are judged on their ability to build and maintain relationships as well as their technical capabilities. And in this instance, they are building their network of sponsors – those who will advocate for them and use their political power to support them.'

'And to maintain those relationships, the leaders need to make time also,' Steve added. 'I think that may be the challenge for many because work can be very busy.'

'Agreed, but people management needs to be treated as highly as other business priorities. If all the people left, the business wouldn't be able to survive. You don't want organisations playing chicken with their employees.'

'Absolutely not, and not just because it is unethical.'

'You raise a good point though, Steve, about leaders needing to be available. It can't just be timetabled. I once knew a project manager, and yes it was a woman, who used to visit her team on Mondays at 10 a.m. She wouldn't come to their building on the same campus any other time. The team didn't like it – it didn't feel authentic.'

'But maybe she had a meeting immediately afterwards and needed input from the team?'

'Perhaps, but it doesn't exactly portray a culture of care. People can pick up inauthenticity very quickly. On the positive side, though, if the team members wanted to speak with her, they knew they would always get an opportunity at 10 a.m. on a Monday.'

'Leadership styles can vary from manager to manager. I remember being told about the Hersey-Blanchard situational leadership model which shows how a leader's approach changes depending on the situation of who they are leading.'

'I think I remember that one. The four-box grid?'

'Yes, that's the one. You start off with *Directing* if your team has low expertise, then as they start learning you move into *Coaching*. Once they become even better, you change again into a more *Supporting* role when and if they need it, and finally once they have all the knowledge and experience needed and are trusted, you can move into *Delegating*.'

'I had a manager once who said he always used a delegatory leadership style.'

'And how did that work out?' Steve asked.

'Not well. What I learned from that experience is if you have a team that is learning or developing skills, a "delegation only" style doesn't work and leaves people feeling lost without clear guidance or vision. And in my case, the manager still wanted to know everything because he clearly didn't trust the team.'

'That's not good. The lack of trust will be visible to the team, and I can tell he didn't inspire you.'

'Is it that obvious?! But thinking about leaders creating leaders, you want organisations to consider how people grow, progress, and move through the organisation. Sometimes that means moving into more senior technical roles and sometimes into leadership roles. So if we look at women in STEM, for example, they have a technical background, but may aspire to be in a leadership role. A bad scenario would be to just put a woman in as the leader without her having any experience or skills to succeed – that's just setting someone up to fail.'

Steve considered this and wrote down some notes. Markus continued.

'Lu, a junior software architect, mentioned hearing her senior managers having a conversation about a woman who had founded a start-up. The woman had just received a significant grant for funding. She told me they made an awful comment: "Oh I don't know how, she's pretty useless." Lu thought there was very much a boy's club with a bit of jealousy or just not thinking that a woman was worth it because she's a woman.'

'I can't say I haven't heard statements like that before. The most important aspect in my view is that people in roles have the skill sets needed to be successful. Just putting someone into a role for optics doesn't work.'

'I agree completely. But what would be better is an organisation identifying a woman as a potential future leader and making sure she gets the training, coaching, mentoring, shadowing, and so on, so that when she gets that leadership position, she is set up for success. A trend I see is that a lot of women do a lot of self-development courses – I don't know if that's related to imposter syndrome though. Anyway, there were a few suggestions during my interviews where women felt men don't put as much focus on their personal development.'

'Is that true though? Or just a perception?' Steve asked.

'It could be a perception, but as I said, it came up a few times. One woman suggested that more experienced men in the industry see themselves in other men coming up and will make suggestions to them on courses or competences that would benefit them. That would be from those men having built effective relationships. She said it was much rarer to find someone who will do that for women.'

'That doesn't happen?'

'I honestly don't know,' Markus replied. 'Many of the women I spoke with mentioned the "broken rung" in stepping up to leadership – it seems to be very difficult for them to make that transition. Another woman I spoke with called Anji shared her experience with her career progression with me where she said she remembered feeling like she was soaring in her technical support role. She said it wasn't that her job was easy – far from it – but she felt she could be herself. All the things she enjoyed – having autonomy, making decisions, making an impact, being creative, mentoring others – were part of her job.'

'That sounds great, but I'm sensing a "but" coming.'

'Yes, unfortunately, it didn't last. She said she developed great relationships with multiple levels of the organisation around the globe and felt valued. But after five years in the role, she started to get bored. She thought it would be straightforward to move to a more challenging position, especially as she had proven herself repeatedly and consistently received great performance ratings. But it didn't happen, and she has now spent the last four years supporting teams with their "office housework".

'That is very disappointing to hear and sounds like a missed opportunity for the business. Did she say what caused it?'

'Only that she moved to a new team who didn't know her and she had to start over by proving herself again.'

'It's a shame that one of those managers from her previous role didn't advocate for her.'

'Agreed, especially as her career progression has stalled now for four years. So that's both sides that make women feel bad at work – we talked about women being artificially promoted to satisfy a quota, which doesn't make anyone feel good, and having a "broken rung", which prevents career progression.'

'I can't imagine anyone would feel positive in either of those situations,' Steve replied. 'I wonder how many women feel stuck in their current role and unable to progress, but still receive top performance ratings…?'

'I suspect there are many. Despite all the shortcomings seen from some leaders, Tara, she's in business development for new energy solutions, said she believes leadership and their mindset is still the missing ingredient for career progression for women.'

***

'What do you think would help with gender equity in this organisation?'

'I think it really helps if the person at the top is neutral,' Tara said. 'They need to know that it's not about men, women, religions, and so on. They need to be more neutral and more accepting.'

'So by neutral, you mean not pushing a specific line of diversity to meet?'

'Yes, so not just pushing gender equity, or neurodiversity, for example. For me, it's about inclusion of everyone and all their differences, but also their similarities. And acknowledging any differences and needs to make sure those with those needs feel just as included as everyone else. Acceptance of diversity flows from the top down – I am sure that will lead to a lot of uncomfortable conversations.'

'And do you think that will help more under-recognised groups to progress through the organisation?'

'Yes, I do – and their progression will be more accepted by everyone because it will be clear that it's not being done to tick a box.'

***

'That is important,' Steve replied. 'And we want leaders who we know will do the right thing for the business as well as their team – and that's every member of their team.'

'Yes, absolutely. Leaders who will not only promote an inclusive culture within their teams but also will advocate for their people when it matters. A sign of a good leader is to create more leaders; therefore, you want these leaders to actively support their team members' career progression.'

'Agreed. Oh, look at the time! Markus, I need to leave sharp today. How about a quick break and then we can sum up the discussion?'

***

Today, work and life are very interconnected, especially with the rise of hybrid and flexible working practices. This is an opportunity for leaders to develop their interpersonal skills by getting to know their colleagues and building authentic and trusting relationships. Leaders who know their junior employees well are in the best position to advocate for them for development opportunities or promotions.

An organisational leader needs to be mindful of the additional challenges that women face and should work with them to provide support when needed. It can be more difficult for women to build relationships with their leaders in the same way as their male counterparts. For this reason, the leader needs to identify effective ways to build as good a relationship with the women in the team as with the men.

Top Tips for Organisations:

- Encourage leaders to get to know their junior employees in order for them to advocate on their behalf for new roles, development opportunities, or performance.

✻ Leaders need to be available to their junior employees to build connections, offer advice on training and shadowing opportunities as well as career coaching.

✻ When identifying women as future leaders, map out a development plan with them to have them set up for success once in a leadership role, and check back with them on progress.

✻ Consider training employees in the use of situational leadership styles prior to appointment as a leader in the organisation.

Top Tips for Women:

✻ Get to know your manager as well as any other key decision makers and make sure they know you, including your skills, development needs, and career aspirations.

✻ Build your network of sponsors who can advocate for you when you are not in the room.

✻ Network with several leaders to gain advice on any gaps in your skill sets and how to close them prior to stepping into a leadership role.

Summary of part 3

Steve and Markus return from their break thinking about all the aspects of leadership they covered during the day. Steve is somewhat distracted and mentions a key meeting he needs to join by phone after he leaves Markus's offices. However, they agree to review their key points and conclude the session slightly earlier than expected.

***

'Well, looks like we got through a lot today, Markus.'

'Yes, we have. Leadership and empowerment is a big topic, and can make a huge difference in people's careers, especially those who don't quite fit the traditional mould.'

'You mean women?'

'Yes, well, it is just more difficult for them while they remain under-recognised in the workplace. You see some people doing really well in organisations, often men but sometimes women, but for others it can be struggle after struggle to be seen, heard, and included.'

'Yes, it can be difficult,' replied Steve. 'Especially given the additional challenges we now have. We've spoken a lot today about leaders getting to know their junior employees, but it is that much harder with remote working and hybrid working becoming the norm. I know it's not impossible to build relationships remotely, but it is so much easier face to face.'

'I know what you mean. In my opinion, you can't beat the coffee room conversations or those before and after meetings where you get a chance to catch up. But being physically present may not always be possible – and we need to guard against bias based on that.'

Steve shook his head. 'How can you see someone as a leader if you don't see them in the room? Sometimes they just need to be physically present.'

'I'm not sure I agree with you, Steve. You can tell what's coming next, right? Only those who come into the offices get the promotions and challenging roles – and that makes the challenge even more difficult for those with responsibilities outside of work – and that's generally women.'

'I understand that, but in today's world of business, people need to be seen and relationships happen in person.'

'I don't have the answer, but what organisations will need to do is to keep talking about this stuff. Keep it high on the agenda. Tackle bias by talking about it. Challenge their leaders on selection of people for the right roles and make sure they're developing their existing workforce at the same time.'

'Yes, they can't afford to fall behind their competitors.'

'Maybe that's a way to help the workforce to understand,' Markus replied. 'Often people talk about managers who make decisions but don't explain the reasoning behind their decisions. It leaves people feeling out of the loop and with very little control of things that may impact them considerably. And unfortunately, this is one way for people to be disengaged, and feel undervalued.'

'Well, then we need to add something about communication. Ensuring the right information is passed on to the workforce to align everyone on the "why" as well as the "what".'

'Yes, exactly that. If all organisations did that, it would definitely make a difference. We need to encourage leaders to make the time for this as we know lack of time squeezes out good communication.'

'Time is often the challenge. But you're right, it's just something that needs to be managed.'

'Another key area of focus is making sure leaders are promoting environments where successes are celebrated and people are not afraid to ask for help without resulting in any negativity towards them. There should also be visible role models who embody the behaviours that the organisation wants to promote.'

'There's a phrase I remember from the awards ceremony last year – "You can't be what you can't see" – role models are a good way to support that,' Steve added.

'Yes, that was the phrase. We want women in the organisations today and those who join in the future to be able to see people who are like them. And we also talked about lifting others as they rise – this can apply to anyone really, but I can see the people that do being the role models.'

'That is one sure way to encourage others to do the same.'

'And the role models may be leaders already – they could be part of the gender affinity network, for example.'

'Then the final part we tackled this afternoon was about sponsors and advocates for women. I'm going to have a few discussions on this with my leadership team when I get back because there may be some things we can do to provide shadowing opportunities as well as testing the robustness of the development plans our people have in place.'

'That's a good idea, Steve – I'm going to encourage the same. I suspect there is always room for improvement.'

'Yes, indeed, Markus. Well, I'd better be heading off now, but I'll see you at the awards ceremony in December. Thank you for your hospitality today.'

***

Once again it appears that Steve is planning to focus his communication with his team who report directly to him rather than more broadly throughout his organisation. He doesn't see this as a problem because he believes that is what his leadership team are for – to manage the "people things" – which is concerning. With this approach, it will be difficult for the women at lower levels of the organisation to know what is happening and what changes are being proposed. When changes are rolled out without consideration of the impact on people, those same people can become very disengaged and untrusting of their leadership.

Markus is very open when it comes to sharing his discussions with women in STEM throughout the year as well as his opinions on Steve's views.

They are continuing to learn a lot from each other and are examples of men navigating today's workplace. They are looking to the future now and how they want their future leaders to behave.

Women in STEM know how to engage, enable, and retain women in STEM. Leaders should consider soliciting feedback from the women in STEM in their organisation to identify improvements in leadership both for those working for leaders, and for those in leadership positions themselves. This is key for any successful progression on gender equity in the organisation.

Conclusion

It is December and the two men once again attend the awards ceremony for women in STEM. This year Markus's organisation is sponsoring one of the award categories. Steve attends and brings one of the junior employees along. Markus spots Steve during one of the networking breaks and makes his way towards him. They catch up and reflect on how much they've learned since they initially met a year ago.

***

'Steve! Great to see you! It's amazing how much we've done since we were here last year.'

'Hello, Markus, yes, that's true! I learned so much from our interactions on recognising and acknowledging behaviours in my organisation, inclusion of women's technical skills and knowledge, and empowerment of future leaders. I know you did a lot of research over the last year and it was great to learn from you and through my own team.'

'I got a lot out of it, too. I learned the difference between "leaning in" and becoming a true ally, and it has made a real difference to me as an individual. Last week I attended a "STEM Day" at my daughter Isabella's school where I spent the day with the kids playing with Lego® and explaining how any of them could go into a STEM career when they grow up if that is what they want to do.'

'That's lovely, Markus, getting to spend time with your daughter and inspire those kids at the same time.'

'I counted up the number of discussions I've had with women in STEM over the last year, both internal and external to my organisation, and it ended up being around 60 – I don't think I even knew 60 women in STEM last year! I have learned a lot about their experiences in the workplace and their examples of best practices to avoid the more negative situations they shared.'

Markus reflected on those best practices he had shared with Steve through their quarterly meetings. He had enjoyed the discussions and challenges from Steve and believes that every person's viewpoint is important as it is informed by their experiences to date. Maybe Steve's challenges could very well represent challenges that someone in his organisation may also encounter.

'I also enjoyed our quarterly meetings – having a day away from the office really helped me to dedicate my thoughts to improving the organisation for women,' replied Steve. 'This year I've been very focused on reducing the attrition of women in the organisation. I want my organisation positioned as an inclusive employer which will increase the innovation in our solutions offered to our customers.'

'That's great, Steve! And how do you feel your organisation has changed in the last year in terms of inclusivity?'

Steve remembered many of Markus's suggestions that he had taken back to his leadership team for a quarterly discussion on diversity and inclusion. Sadly, he felt there had been some great ideas to move forward, but due to it being so busy, many of the ideas were deprioritised until more people were available to support and deliver them.

'Well, I know I have kept my Fridays clear of regularly scheduled meetings – to keep me available if anyone in the team would like a chat. Also, I had eight meetings with women in STEM over the last year – that's two a quarter. I have also been challenging my leadership team on some of the statements made by the women describing their experiences. I want my team to define how to correct the issues, as I want them to fully support what needs to be done.'

'That's exactly how I would do it, too. You need their buy-in.'

'Yes, that is key. And I don't know if you've heard – my manager has elected to retire and I have been named the new CEO effective 1st January.'

'Congratulations, Steve – that is fantastic news! Even more so having a CEO who is very passionate about gender equity in STEM.'

Steve waved over his colleague and introduced Markus to Fergus.

'Fergus has worked for me for a number of years and will step into my current role once I become CEO. However, effective immediately, I have delegated all gender equity initiatives to Fergus. I don't see me having the capacity to drive these activities once I am in my new role.'

Markus paused and wondered exactly how 'hands-off' Steve would become.

Steve continued, 'Fergus is excellent, and always delivers great work. Our regular check-ins are always positive, and

I know Fergus is someone I can rely on. Thank you for the check-ins this year, Markus – they have been incredibly insightful. Going forward, though, I will be handing these over to Fergus. Well, I best be going, but I wish you both all the best.'

Markus thought back to March where he remembered Steve describing one of his direct reports who seemed to always say what his management wanted to hear, but potentially his own direct reports would describe their experiences differently. Fergus reminded Markus of that 'James'. Surely this wasn't the person to take over an initiative as important as this?

'Nice to meet you, Fergus,' replied Markus, 'and I hope to learn as much from you as I have from Steve over the last year.'

'Great to meet you, too, Markus. Steve speaks very highly of you. I am very excited about looking into gender equity initiatives within our organisation.'

'Have you been involved in any initiatives like this previously?'

'No, this is all new to me, but I'm very much looking forward to it.'

'Not to worry, we all have to start somewhere. Do you know how the women in STEM feel in your organisation?'

'Oh, they love working there and they are trailblazers for women in STEM. Our organisation is very much ticking the diversity box!'

Markus was a little surprised and wondered how much Fergus and Steve had discussed.

'My organisation still has some way to go in our journey, but I'm happy to share thoughts and advice with you, Fergus.'

'That's great, but my number one focus for next year is recruitment of more women in STEM as we want to hit our quotas.'

Two men from other companies join their conversation. Markus shares his story of how he and Steve met the previous year and had arranged quarterly reciprocal mentoring sessions to discuss how to improve the experiences of women within their respective organisations. Fergus and the other two men like this idea and commit to a similar reciprocal mentoring programme to start their own journeys to ensure the women in STEM feel valued at work. Markus commits to continuing his own path towards engaging and retaining women and enabling opportunities for them to progress within their companies.

***

Markus and Steve have spent a year sharing experiences and advice on gender equity for women in STEM. They have had contrasting approaches, and in the end, their paths diverged.

Steve never made the progression to 'leaning in' and has now delegated his accountabilities for gender equity to Fergus. This is not encouraging, as Fergus is focused on meeting quotas and looking good in front of Steve. Markus, on the other hand, has driven creation of a new reciprocal mentoring group, where the number of organisations included has now doubled. He has taken part in initiatives outside of his workplace, and continues to be driven by his wish to have an equitable workplace culture for Isabella. This kind of drive is authentic and will persevere when challenges arise.

Markus is a role model for male leaders in traditionally male-dominated organisations. He is not perfect, but he tries, and approaches this with curiosity, openness, and respect. Markus is open to receiving constructive feedback to make his actions more effective for sustainable change. This year Markus has been fact-finding, but next year he will progress even further by sponsoring his organisation's ERG and securing a budget for more impactful and inclusive initiatives and events.

If in doubt, when considering shining a light on bias to engage, enable, and retain women in STEM in male-dominated industries, be like Markus.

Call to action

Women in STEM have a clear role in solving today's and tomorrow's challenges, but not everyone is at a level in the organisation to make it happen.

To access additional resources to support driving change at various levels within your organisation, please visit:

www.valuedatwork.com

And if you would like a more bespoke solution that may include workshop design and facilitation, keynote speaking, or 1-2-1 coaching, please email us at:

connect@valuedatwork.com

Let's change these workplace cultures to ensure women in STEM truly feel valued at work to reach their potential and make a positive difference in the world!

And who knows? Maybe those women will be recognisable role models to inspire future generations.

About the author

Lauren Neal is a champion of gender equity and career progression within STEM.

She is a chartered engineer through the Institution of Engineering and Technology (IET), a chartered project professional through the Association for Project Management, a member of the Chartered Management Institute, and a certified International Consortium for Agile (ICAgile) team facilitator and coach, with a focus on improving team dynamics.

Originally from Aberdeen, Scotland, Lauren was named one of the UK's top female computing students at age 18. She went on to gain a Master's in Electronic and Electrical Engineering, and since 2005, has worked offshore, onshore, and on-site on multimillion-dollar projects across the UK, Angola, Trinidad, Azerbaijan, and Indonesia.

A STEM ambassador and tutor in mathematics, Lauren is a former chair of the IET Scotland North Younger Members group, and chaired her organisation's regional Women's International Network business resource group and the Women in Projects initiative during a five-year assignment to Azerbaijan.

Lauren is a winner of WeAreTheCity's 2022 Rising Stars award in the Energy & Utilities category, WeAreTechWomen's 2022 TechWomen100 winner, and was named in Diverse In's 2022 '130 Women Who Break the Bias List'.

She writes and speaks regularly on gender equity.

Bibliography

A. Benson, D. Li, and K. Shue, *'Potential' and the Gender Pay Promotion Gap* (2022). Available from: https://danielle-li.github.io/assets/docs/PotentialAndTheGenderPromotionGap.pdf [accessed 30 December 2022].

R. Billan, *Successful Women Pay a Price*, Forbes (2019). Available from: www.forbes.com/sites/rumeetbillan/2019/03/06/the-tallest-poppy/ [accessed 1 January 2023].

S. Braiden, *Ask These 7 Questions to Boost Psychological Safety at Work*, IHUBApp (2020). Available from: www.inspirehub.com/blog/ask-these-7-questions-to-boost-psychological-safety-at-work [accessed 26 December 2022]

Cairnie, R. and O. Muscat, *Cultivating Female Talent in Energy: what the sector can do to resolve the barriers faced by women in middle management*, POWERful Women and Bain & Company (2022). Available from: www.bain.com/contentassets/56020f4e0325412c95b66602ae9a2064/cultivating-female-talent-in-energy_pfw-bain_april-2022-final_2-1.pdf [accessed 13 September 2022].

L. Davey, 'Deliver Feedback That Sticks', *Harvard Business Review* (2015). Available from: https://hbr.org/2015/08/deliver-feedback-that-sticks [accessed 30 December 2022].

F. Gino and K. Coffman, 'Unconscious Bias Training That Works', *Harvard Business Review* (2021). Available from: https://hbr.org/2021/09/unconscious-bias-training-that-works [accessed 30 December 2022].

P. Hersey and K. Blanchard, 'Life Cycle Theory of Leadership' in *Training and Development Journal*, 23(2), 26–34 (1969).

International Energy Agency (IEA), *IEA World Energy Employment Report*, International Energy Agency (IEA), Paris (2022). Available from: www.iea.org/reports/world-energy-employment [accessed 13 September 2022].

LeanIn.Org and McKinsey, *Women in the Workplace 2022*, LeanIn.Org and McKinsey (2022). Available from: https://wiw-report.s3.amazonaws.com/Women_in_the_Workplace_2022.pdf [accessed 13 September 2022].

K. Ludeman and E. Erlandson, 'Coaching the Alpha Male', *Harvard Business Review* (2004). Available from: https://hbr.org/2004/05/coaching-the-alpha-male [accessed 28 December 2022].

Men Leaning In Matrix, Potentia Talent Consulting Limited, Token Man Consulting (2022). Available from: https://docs.google.com/presentation/d/1OovRRKb3LbXDdLYZsMnixuugz74FtjJpU8-sBXc5nGg/edit#slide=id.g184f34ba142_1_387 [accessed 2 January 2023].

Pantene, 'Labels Against Women' Digital Ad (2013). Available from: www.youtube.com/watch?v=luLkfXixBpM [accessed 30 December 2022].

S. Sandberg, *Lean In: Women, Work, and the Will to Lead*, W
H Allen (2015). [Sheryl Sandberg's comment on a Hewlett
Packard internal report, p. 62].

US Census Bureau, *Women Are Nearly Half of U.S. Workforce
but Only 27 % of STEM Workers. Women Making Gains in
STEM Occupations but Still Underrepresented*, United States
Census Bureau [A. Martinez and C. Christnacht] (2021).
Available from: www.census.gov/library/stories/2021/01/
women-making-gains-in-stem-occupations-but-still-
underrepresented.html [accessed 13 September 2022].

U. Von Lonski, et al. *Untapped Reserves 2.0: Driving Gender
Balance in Oil and Gas*, Boston Consulting Group and World
Petroleum Council (2021). Available from: www.bcg.com/
publications/2021/gender-diversity-in-oil-gas-industry
[accessed 13 September 2022].

WISE, *Updated Workforce Statistics – June 2022*, Women into
Science and Engineering (WISE) (2022). Available from:
www.wisecampaign.org.uk/updated-workforce-statistics-
june-2022/ [accessed 13 September 2023].

Index

A quick word from Practical Inspiration Publishing...

We hope you found this book both practical and inspiring – that's what we aim for with every book we publish.

We publish titles on topics ranging from leadership, entrepreneurship, HR and marketing to self-development and wellbeing.

Find details of all our books at: www.practicalinspiration.com

 Did you know...

We can offer discounts on bulk sales of all our titles – ideal if you want to use them for training purposes, corporate giveaways or simply because you feel these ideas deserve to be shared with your network.

We can even produce bespoke versions of our books, for example with your organization's logo and/or a tailored foreword.

To discuss further, contact us on info@practicalinspiration.com.

 Got an idea for a business book?

We may be able to help. Find out more about publishing in partnership with us at: bit.ly/PIpublishing.

Follow us on social media...

 @PIPTalking

@pip_talking

@practicalinspiration

@piptalking

Practical Inspiration Publishing

Milton Keynes UK
Ingram Content Group UK Ltd.
UKHW022158290923
429657UK00006B/231

9 781788 605601